1001
Most Useful
SPANISH
Words
NEW EDITION

Pablo García Loaeza, Ph.D.

DOVER PUBLICATIONS, INC.
Mineola, New York

Copyright

Copyright © 2013 by Dover Publications, Inc.
Text copyright © 2010 by Pablo García Loaeza, Ph.D.
All rights reserved.

Bibliographical Note

1001 Most Useful Spanish Words NEW EDITION, first published by Dover Publications, Inc., in 2013, is a new selection of material from *2,001 Most Useful Spanish Words*, published in 2010 by Dover Publications, Inc.

Library of Congress Cataloging-in-Publication Data

Loaeza, Pablo García, 1972–
     1001 most useful Spanish words / Pablo García Loaeza.—New ed.
         p. cm.—
     "1001 Most Useful Spanish Words New ed., first published
by Dover Publications, Inc., in 2013, is a new selection of material
from 2,001 Most Useful Spanish Words, published in 2010 by Dover
Publications, Inc."
     ISBN-13: 978-0-486-49899-7—ISBN-10: 0-486-49899-9
         1. Spanish language—Vocabulary.   2. Spanish language—
Usage.   3. Spanish language—Grammar.   I. Title.   II. Title: One
thousand and one most useful Spanish words.   III. Title: 2,001 most
useful Spanish words.
PC4445.L623 2013
468.2'421—dc23

                                                                2012021716

Manufactured in the United States by Courier Corporation
49899901
www.doverpublications.com

Contents

Introduction

This book contains well over one thousand useful Spanish words for general communication and everyday situations. It was designed as a self-teaching tool that can also be used for reference and review. In the first section of the book each alphabetically-ordered word entry includes a sentence in Spanish (and its English translation) that shows how a word might be used. An m. or an f. after a noun indicates whether it is masculine or feminine; the abbreviation pl. stands for plural. Many of the entries include a noun or adjective in parentheses to show the versatility of a specific word. In the second part of the book you will find words grouped by categories. These are very common words whose context is self-evident such as numbers, colors, stores, and days of the week; they are not repeated in the alphabetical section. The book takes into account Spanish dialectical variation by including words used in Spain (Sp.) and Latin America, Mexico, Argentina (L. Am., Mex., Arg., etc.).

Vocabulary is best acquired in context and through frequent repetition. When you study the words in this book, picture yourself in the situations in which you might use them. The sentences provided will help you to imagine an appropriate context. Say them out loud to practice hearing and producing the sounds of Spanish. The more familiar they become, the easier it will be for you to understand and be understood when speaking with others. Use the words you learn as often as you can so that they "stick" and become your own.

The illustrative sentences are deliberately simple. As you study a word in a sentence, look at the words around it to discover the way Spanish is structured. In time, you will learn to recognize several basic structures and rely increasingly less on the English translation. After a while, cover the English sentences with a sheet of paper, try to figure out the meaning of the Spanish sentences on your own, and then uncover the English version to check for accuracy. With some practice you will find that your translation is correct more often than not.

While practice is always the best way to master a language, many people may find Dover's *Essential Spanish Grammar* (0-486-20780-3) helpful. Likewise, the *1001 Easy Spanish Phrases* (0-486-47619-7), also published by Dover, is a useful complement for increasing your dexterity in Spanish.

A Note on Spanish Dialects

As with English, there are many regional dialects of Spanish. They may vary in pronunciation, vocabulary, and syntax but they are all mutually intelligible.

For instance, in the Castile region of Spain a "c" before an "e" or an "i" sounds like "th" in English and the letter "s" is pronounced like "sh." On the other hand, people in the south of Spain and in Latin America, generally make the letter "c" (before "e" or "i"), the letter "s," and even the letter "z" all sound like the "s" in "soup." Caribbean Spanish tends to drop a "d" between two vowels at the end of some words, as well as a final "s" so that *cansados* (tired, m. pl.) becomes *cansao*. Likewise, in many South-American countries the word for cake is *torta*, whereas in Mexico it is *pastel*. In Latin America a computer is called *una computadora* while in Spain it is referred to as *un ordenador*. Nevertheless, a Spaniard, a Mexican, a Chilean, and a Dominican can engage in conversation without impediment.

When Spanish is learned as a second language the choice of dialect can depend on personal interest and circumstance. For example, someone traveling to Spain might prefer to become familiar with the Castilian dialect, while someone spending time in a Latin American country will pick up the local accent and lingo. The best investment for a beginner studying stateside is to practice a "neutral" kind of Spanish: all the syllables in a word should be pronounced clearly, using the standard word-stress rules (see below). Once you know the basic rules, a little practice makes it easy to compensate for dialectical differences. Remember also that the most useful words, such as *por favor* and *gracias*, are the same throughout the Spanish-speaking world.

Unlike English—in which the same word may be written one way in Britain (colour, dialogue, emphasise, gaol) and another in the United States (color, dialog, emphasize, jail)—all Spanish dialects use the same written standard.

Spanish Pronunciation Guide

Vowels

Spanish only has five vowel sounds (English has over 15!) which correspond to the five vowel letters, regardless of their position in a word. There are no silent vowels in Spanish. The five vowel sounds in Spanish are:

a as in dr**a**ma   *Habla a la casa blanca.*   Call the White House.
e as in b**e**t   *Él es el rebelde René Pérez.*   He is the rebel René Pérez.
i as in d**ee**p   *Sí, viví sin ti.*   Yes, I lived without you.
o as in c**oa**t   *Los locos no son tontos.*   Crazy people aren't dumb.
u as in l**oo**p   *Fui a un club nocturno.*   I went to a nightclub.

The semi-consonant **y** is pronounced like **i** [ee] when used as a conjunction: Pedro **y** María (*Pedro* **and** *María*); its sound softens next to a vowel (as in **y**ellow): Juan y **y**o somos muy buenos amigos (*Juan and I are very good friends*).

Consonants

Spanish has basically the same consonant sounds as English. However, there are a few particulars to keep in mind:

b and **v** are very often pronounced the same way as in "bee."
c (soft), **s**, and **z** vary in pronunciation in some Spanish dialects. However, in all but the rarest cases, they can all be pronounced like the **s** in "soft" without risk of confusion.
g is hard as in **g**ood before **a**, **o**, and **u**, but soft as the **h** in **h**orse before **e** or **i**.
gu is used before **e** and **i** to represent a soft **g** sound as in **g**ood (note that here the **u** does not function as a vowel; **gu** is a digraph in which two letters represent a single sound as in **th**e)
h is always mute as in **h**erbs.
j is pronounced like the **h** in **h**orse.
ll is always pronounced like **y** as in **y**ellow.
ñ represents a particular sound which resembles the **ny** combination found in ca**ny**on or barn**y**ard.
qu is used before **e** and **i** to represent a hard **c** sound as in **c**at (see **gu** above)

r at the beginning of a word is trilled.
rr represents a trill in the middle of a word.

Stress and written accents

Spanish words tend to have two or more syllables; when they are pronounced one syllable always sounds a little bit louder than the others. The stressed syllable is either the last, the next to last (most often), or the second to last syllable (least often). Word stress in Spanish is determined by two simple rules:

1. Words that end in a **vowel**, **n**, or **s** are generally pronounced stressing the **next to last syllable**:
   Ven**ta**na (*window*), **bar**co (*boat*), pa**lab**ras (*words*), tú **can**tas (*you sing*), ellos **com**en (*they eat*)
2. Words which end in a **consonant** other than **n** or **s** are generally stressed on the **last syllable**:
   pa**pel** (*paper*), fe**liz** (*happy*), acti**tud** (*attitude*), can**tar** (*to sing*), com**er** (*to eat*)

Written accent marks indicate a stress where you wouldn't normally expect it:
   can**ción** (*song*), él can**tó** (*he sang*),[1] **lá**piz (*pencil*), a**zú**car (*sugar*), mur**ci**élago (*bat*)[2], **cír**culo (*circle*)

---

[1] Note the difference with yo **can**to (*I sing*): a change in stress can significantly change the meaning of a word or even a whole sentence.
[2] Repeating the word **murciélago** out loud is a good way to practice pronunciation: it has all five vowel sounds and distinctive stress.

Alphabetical Section

A

a (tiempo, veces)   *to, on time, some times*
A veces salgo a comer y trato de llegar a tiempo.
Sometimes I go out to eat and I try to be on time.

a través   *across, through*
Muchas cosas han cambiado a través de los años.
Many things have changed through the years.

abajo (de)   *under, down*
La maleta está abajo.
The suitcase is downstairs.

abierto/-a   *open*
La farmacia está abierta.
The drugstore is open.

acabar   *to finish*
Acaba tu tarea antes de irte.
Finish your homework before you leave.

accidente m.   *accident*
Por suerte, el accidente no fue grave.
Luckily, the accident wasn't serious.

aceptar   *to accept*
¿Aceptan tarjetas de crédito?
Do you accept credit cards?

aconsejar   *to advise, to recommend*
Te aconsejo usar crema solar en la playa.
I recommend you use sunscreen at the beach.

acordarse   *to remember*
Siempre me acordaré de ti.
I will always remember you.

acuerdo m.   *agreement*
Todos firmaron el acuerdo.
Everyone signed the agreement.

adaptador m.   *adaptor*
¿Dónde puedo comprar un adaptador de corriente?
Where can I buy a power adaptor?

adentro m.   *inside, within*
Vamos adentro.
Let's go inside.

adiós   *good-bye*
Es triste tener que decir adiós.
It's sad to have to say good-bye.

admirar   *to admire*
Quiero admirar la vista desde aquí.
I want to admire the view from here.

aduana f.   *customs*
Al llegar, debemos pasar por la aduana.
On arrival, we have to go through customs.

advertir   *to warn*
Le advertí que no lo hiciera.
I warned him not to do it.

aeropuerto m.   *airport*
El aeropuerto está cerca de la ciudad.
The airport is near the city.

aficionado m.   *fan, amateur*
Soy un aficionado del fútbol americano.
I am a fan of football.

afuera   *outside*
¿Hace frío afuera?
Is it cold outside?

agencia (de viajes) f.   *(travel) agency*
¿Sabe dónde está la agencia de viajes más cercana?
Do you know where the nearest travel agency is?

agradable   *pleasant*
Las noches de verano son muy agradables aquí.
Summer nights are very pleasant here.

agradecer   *to thank*
Le agradezco su amabilidad.
I thank you for your kindness.

aguja f.   *needle*
Necesito aguja e hilo para arreglar mi vestido.
I need needle and thread to mend my dress.

ahora (mismo)   *right now*
Debemos salir ahora mismo para llegar a tiempo.
We must leave right now to be on time.

ahorrar   *to save*
Queremos ahorrar dinero.
We want to save money.

al fin   *finally*
Nos perdimos, pero al fin llegamos.
We got lost, but we finally made it.

al lado de   *next to*
Mi oficina está al lado de la tuya.
My office is next to yours.

alegrar(se)   *to make someone happy*
Me alegra verte.
I'm happy to see you.

alérgico/-a   *allergic*
Soy alérgico a los camarones.
I am allergic to shrimp.

algo   *something*
¿Quieres algo de comer?
Do you want something to eat?

algodón m.   *cotton*
Quiero comprar unas camisas de algodón.
I want to buy some cotton shirts.

alguien   *somebody, someone*
¿Me llamó alguien por teléfono?
Did someone call me on the phone?

algún, alguno/-a(s)   *some*
A algunas personas no les gusta viajar.
Some people don't like to travel.

alimentar(se)   *to feed, to eat*
Es necesario alimentarse bien para tener energía.
It is necessary to eat well to have energy.

aliviar   *to relieve, to alleviate*
¿Quieres algo para aliviar el dolor?
Do you want something to relieve the pain?

allí/allá   *there/over there*
¿Qué es eso que está allá?
What's that over there?

almorzar   *to have lunch*
¿Me puede recomendar un lugar para almorzar?
Can you recommend a place to have lunch?

alojamiento m.   *lodging*
Estoy buscando alojamiento para mis vacaciones.
I am looking for lodging for my vacation.

alto   *stop*
Una luz roja significa hacer un alto
A red light means to stop.

alto/-a   *tall, high*
¡Qué montaña tan alta!
What a tall mountain!

amable   *kind*
Miguel es una persona muy amable.
Miguel is a very kind person.

amar(se)   *to love (each other)*
Yo te amo y tú amas la música.
I love you and you love music.

ambos   *both*
Ambos trenes llegaron al mismo tiempo.
Both trains arrived at the same time.

ambulancia f.   *ambulance*
¡Alguien llame una ambulancia!
Somebody call an ambulance!

amigo/-a m./f.   *friend*
María es una buena amiga mía.
Maria is a good friend of mine.

amistad f.   *friendship*
La amistad es verdaderamente una gran cosa.
Friendship is truly a great thing.

amor m.   *love*
El amor verdadero es difícil de encontrar.
True love is hard to find.

ancho/-a   *wide, broad*
El río amazonas es muy ancho.
The Amazon River is very wide.

andar   *to go, to walk*
Me gustaría andar por el centro de la ciudad.
I would like to walk around downtown.

anteojos m. pl.   *eyeglasses*
No puedo ver nada sin mis anteojos.
I cannot see a thing without my eyeglasses.

anterior   *the one before, the previous one*
Este libro es mejor que el anterior.
This book is better than the previous one.

antes   *before*
Es importante lavarse las manos antes de comer.
It's important to wash one's hands before eating.

antiguo/-a   *ancient/old*
La cultura azteca es muy antigua.
Aztec culture is very old.

antipático/-a   *unfriendly, unkind*
El mesero que nos atendió era muy antipático.
The waiter who took care of us was very unfriendly.

anular   *to cancel*
Anulé mi cita con el doctor.
I canceled my doctor's appointment.

apagar   *to turn off*
Por favor, apaga el radio.
Please, turn off the radio.

aparecer   *to appear*
Las estrellas aparecieron en el cielo.
The stars appeared in the sky.

apellido m.   *family name, last name*
Mi apellido es Bond.
My last name is Bond.

apoyar(se)   *to lean on/support*
Puedes apoyarte en mí.
You can lean on me.

aprender (de memoria)   *to learn (by heart)*
Quiero aprender a bailar tango.
I want to learn to dance the tango.

apresurar(se)   *to hurry*
Apresúrate, se nos hace tarde.
Hurry up, it's getting late.

aquí/acá   *here/over here*
¡Ven para acá ahora mismo!
Come over here right now!

árbol m.   *tree*
Quiero descansar a la sombra de un árbol.
I want to rest under the shade of a tree.

archivo m.   *file*
Los archivos están guardados en el disco duro de mi computadora.
The files are stored on the hard drive of my computer.

arreglar   *to fix, to arrange*
¿Quién nos puede arreglar el auto?
Who can fix our car for us?

arriba   *up*
Mira hacia arriba.
Look up.

ascensor m.   *elevator*
El edificio tiene dos ascensores.
The building has two elevators.

asco m.   *disgust*
Siento asco por ese mal olor.
That bad smell disgusts me.

asegurar(se)   *to insure, to secure, to make sure*
Asegúrate de no olvidar nada.
Make sure you're not forgetting anything.

así   *thus, this way*
Mira, es mejor hacerlo así.
Look, it's better to do it this way.

asiento (para bebé) m.   *(child) seat*
¿Está ocupado este asiento?
Is this seat taken?

asistir (a)   *to attend*
Quiero asistir al concierto esta noche.
I want to attend the concert tonight.

asunto m.   *matter, subject*
El calentamiento global es un asunto importante.
Global warming is an important matter.

atención f.   *attention*
¿Estás prestando atención?
Are you paying attention?

atender   *to tend to, to take care of*
Un buen médico atiende a sus pacientes.
A good doctor takes care of his patients.

atrás   *behind*
Da un paso atrás.
Take a step back.

aumentar   *to increase*
El precio del dólar ha aumentado recientemente.
The (currency) exchange rate has increased recently.

aún   *yet, still*
El tren no ha llegado aún.
The train has not arrived yet.

aunque   *although, even though*
La excursión tuvo lugar aunque estaba lloviendo.
The excursion took place even though it was raining.

ausencia f.   *absence*
Nadie notó mi ausencia.
Nobody noticed my absence.

autobús m.   *bus*
¿Se puede llegar allá en autobús?
Can you get there by bus?

automóvil m.   *car, automobile*
Me gustaría rentar un automóvil.
I would like to rent a car.

avenida f.   *avenue*
Hay muchas tiendas en la avenida principal.
There are a lot of stores on the main avenue.

averiguar   *to find out*
Me gustaría averiguar a qué hora abre el museo.
I would like to find out what time the museum opens.

avión m.   *airplane*
Viajaré a España en avión.
I will travel to Spain by airplane.

avisar   *to inform, to warn*
Pedro me avisó que llegaría tarde.
Pedro informed me that he would be late.

aviso m.   *warning, sign*
Debemos hacer caso de los avisos.
We must pay attention to the signs.

ayudar   *to help*
Por favor ayúdame.
Please help me.

B

bailar   *to dance*
¿Quiere bailar?
Would you like to dance?

bajar   *to lower, to go down, to descend*
¡Bajen a cenar!
Come down to eat dinner!

bajo/-a   *low*
¿Cuál es el precio más bajo por este anillo?
What is the lowest price for this ring?

bañar(se)   *to bathe, to take a bath*
Me baño todos los días.
I take a bath every day.

bandera f.   *flag*
¿Cuáles son los colores de la bandera nacional de este país?
What are the colors of this country's national flag?

baño m.   *bathroom*
El baño en este departamento es muy pequeño.
The bathroom in this apartment is very small.

barato/-a   *cheap*
Compré un reloj muy barato; sólo me costó $10 dólares.
I bought a very cheap watch; it was only $10 dollars.

barrio m.   *neighborhood*
Este es un barrio muy agradable.
This is a very nice neighborhood.

base (de datos) f.   *(data)base*
En cualquier negocio es una buena idea tener una base de datos.
In any business it is a good idea to have a database.

bastante   *enough*
¿Dormiste bastante anoche?
Did you sleep enough last night?

basura f.   *garbage, trash*
La basura es un gran problema en las ciudades grandes.
Garbage is a big problem in big cities.

bebé m. & f.   *baby*
¡Qué lindo bebé!
What a cute baby!

beber   *to drink*
Me gusta beber vino tinto.
I like to drink red wine.

beso m.   *kiss*
En muchos países la gente se saluda con un beso.
In many countries people greet each other with a kiss.

bien (hecho)   *well (done)*
Este es un trabajo bien hecho.
This is a job well done.

bienestar m.   *well-being*
La salud es importante para el bienestar de una persona.
Health is important for a person's well-being.

bienvenido/-a   *welcome*
¡Bienvenidos a nuestra casa!
Welcome to our house!

billete m.   *banknote/ticket*
Compraré los billetes para el teatro esta tarde.
I will buy the tickets for the theater this evening.

billetera f.   *wallet*
Alguien me robó mi billetera.
Somebody stole my wallet.

blando/-a   *soft*
Este sillón es muy blando.
This couch is very soft.

boda f.   *wedding*
La boda será en la iglesia.
The wedding will be at the church.

boleto (de ida y vuelta) m.   *(round trip) ticket*
Compraré los boletos para la opera mañana en la mañana.
I will buy the tickets for the opera tomorrow morning.

bolígrafo m.   *ballpoint pen*
Préstame tu bolígrafo para firmar estos documentos.
Lend me your ballpoint pen to sign these documents.

bolsa f.   *bag, purse*
No guardes tu pasaporte en tu bolsa.
Don't keep your passport in your bag.

bonito/-a   *pretty*
Laura es una mujer bonita.
Laura is a pretty woman.

bueno/-a, buen (rato)   *good (time)*
Pasé algunos buenos ratos en Sevilla.
I had some good times in Seville.

buscar   *to look for*
Estoy buscando un restaurante barato.
I am looking for a cheap restaurant.

C

caballero m.   *gentleman*
Ernesto es un verdadero caballero.
Ernesto is a true gentleman.

caber   *to fit (in)*
Toda esa ropa no va a caber en tu maleta.
All those clothes won't fit in your suitcase.

cada   *each*
Hay vuelos que salen cada hora.
There are flights leaving each hour.

caduco/-a   *expired/out-of-date*
Esta medicina está caduca.
This medicine is expired.

caer(se)   *to fall (down)*
Se tropezó y se cayó.
He tripped and fell down.

café m.   *coffee shop/coffee*
Te veré en el café.
I will see you at the coffee shop.

caja (de ahorros) f.   *box, savings bank*
Es mejor guardar el dinero en una caja de ahorros que en una caja de zapatos.
It is better to keep money in a savings bank than in a shoe box.

cajero (automático) m.   *cashier, ATM machine*
Paga la cuenta en el cajero.
Pay the bill with the cashier.

calculadora f.   *calculator*
¿Tienes una calculadora que puedes prestarme?
Do you have a calculator I can borrow?

calendario m.   *calendar*
Según el calendario, hoy es el primero de enero.
According to the calendar, today is January first.

calentar(se)   *to warm, to heat (up)*
Me caliento cerca de la chimenea.
I warm up near the chimney.

caliente *hot*
No me gusta la sopa demasiado caliente.
I don't like soup too hot.

calle f. *street*
Es mejor caminar por el lado sombreado de la calle.
It is better to walk on the shady side of the street.

calmar(se) *to calm (down)*
¡Cálmese!
Calm down!

calor m. *heat, warmth*
Hoy hace mucho calor afuera.
Today it's very hot outside.

cama (doble) f. *(double) bed*
Quiero una habitación con una cama doble.
I want a room with a double bed.

cámara (fotográfica) f. *camera*
Se me olvidó mi cámara.
I forgot my camera.

camarero/-a m./f. *waiter, waitress*
Camarero, mi cuenta por favor.
Waiter, my check please.

cambiar (un cheque) *to change, to exchange, to cash a check*
¿Puede cambiarme este cheque de viajero?
Can you cash this traveler's check for me?

cambio m. *change/cash*
Necesito cambio para dar propinas.
I need change to give tips.

caminar *to walk*
Me gusta caminar por el parque.
I like to walk through the park.

camino m. *road*
¿Es este el camino correcto?
Is this the right road?

camisa f. *shirt*
¿Tiene camisas de algodón?
Do you have cotton shirts?

cáncer m.   *cancer*
Ha habido avances significativos en el tratamiento contra el cáncer.
There have been significant advances in cancer treatment.

canción f.   *song*
Me gustan las canciones tradicionales.
I like traditional songs.

cansado/-a   *tired*
Estoy muy cansado.
I am very tired.

cantar   *to sing*
Siempre canto en la regadera.
I always sing in the shower.

cariñoso/-a   *affectionate*
Los perros suelen ser más cariñosos que los gatos.
Dogs are generally more affectionate than cats.

caro/-a   *expensive*
Estos zapatos son demasiado caros.
These shoes are too expensive.

carretera f.   *highway*
Tomemos la carretera panorámica.
Let's take the scenic highway.

carro (rentado) m.   *(rental) car*
Un carro rentado es más económico que pagar taxis.
A rental car is cheaper than paying for taxis.

carta(s) f.   *letter, menu, playing cards*
Mesero, ¿me permite la carta?
Waiter, may I have the menu?

casa (de campo, editorial) f.   *(country, publishing) house*
Elena trabaja en una casa editorial y tiene una casa de campo.
Elena works in a publishing house and has a country house.

casado/-a   *married*
Luisa y Jerónimo están casados.
Luisa and Jerónimo are married.

casi   *almost*
El tren casi siempre sale a tiempo.
The train almost always leaves on time.

causar   *to cause*
Los huracanes causan grandes daños en el Caribe.
Hurricanes cause great damage in the Caribbean.

celebración f.   *celebration*
El día de la independencia es una celebración nacional.
Independence Day is a national celebration.

cenar   *to eat dinner*
En España la gente cena muy tarde.
In Spain people eat dinner very late.

centro (comercial) m.   *center, downtown/mall*
¿Quieres ir a pasear al centro o prefieres ir al centro comercial?
Do you want to go walk downtown or would you prefer going to the mall?

cercano/-a   *close, near*
¿Dónde está el hospital más cercano?
Where is the nearest hospital?

cerrado/-a   *closed*
Los museos están cerrados los lunes.
Museums are closed on Mondays.

cerrar   *to close*
Por favor cierra la puerta cuando te vayas.
Please close the door when you leave.

cesar   *to stop, to cease*
Los invitados no cesaron de bailar en toda la noche.
The guests didn't stop dancing all night long.

checar   *to check*
Deberíamos checar el aceite del coche antes de salir.
We should check the motor oil before leaving.

cheque (de viajero) m.   *(traveler's) check*
Es más seguro viajar con cheques de viajero.
It is safer to travel with traveler's checks.

cibercafé m.   *Internet café*
¿Sabes dónde puedo encontrar un cibercafé?
Do you know where I can find an Internet café?

cielo m.   *sky*
¡Qué cielo tan azul!
What a blue sky!

cierto/-a   *true, certain*
¡Eso no es cierto!
That is not true!

cine m.   *cinema, movie theater*
¿Quieres ir al cine?
Do you want to go to the movies?

cinta f.   *tape*
Necesito un pedazo de cinta adhesiva.
I need a piece of adhesive tape.

cinturón (de seguridad) m.   *(seat) belt*
Es importante usar cinturones de seguridad.
It's important to wear seat belts.

cita f.   *appointment, date (social)*
Tengo una cita muy importante.
I have a very important appointment.

ciudad f.   *city*
La Ciudad de México es una ciudad enorme.
Mexico City is a huge city.

ciudadano/-a m./f.   *citizen*
Yo soy ciudadano de los Estados Unidos.
I am a United States citizen.

claro/-a   *clear, of course*
¿Quieres un café? ¡Claro!
Would you like a cup of coffee? Of course!

clase f.   *class*
Necesito ir a mi clase de español.
I have to go to my Spanish class.

cobrar   *to charge*
Cobran una cuota para entrar.
They charge a fee to get in.

coche (de alquiler) m.   *(rental) car*
Vine en un coche de alquiler.
I came in a rental car.

cocina f.   *kitchen, cooking, cuisine*
Me encanta la cocina española.
I love Spanish cuisine.

cocinar   *to cook*
Sofía está cocinando la cena en la cocina.
Sofía is cooking dinner in the kitchen.

código (postal) m.   *(postal/zip) code*
Siempre debes escribir el código postal en el sobre.
You must always write the postal code on the envelope.

coger   *to grab, to take*
Coge un paraguas por si llueve.
Grab an umbrella in case it rains.

colección f.   *collection*
El museo está mostrando una interesante colección de pintura.
The museum is showing an interesting painting collection.

comentar   *to comment*
No comentaré sobre el asunto.
I will not comment on the matter.

comenzar   *to begin, to start*
El curso comienza el año próximo.
The course begins next year.

comer   *to eat, to have lunch*
Quiero algo de comer, por favor.
I would like something to eat, please.

comisaría f.   *police station*
Lo llevaron a la comisaría.
They took him to the police station.

como   *like, as*
Lo quiero como a un hermano.
I love him like a brother.

cómodo/-a   (as adj.) *comfortable*
Me siento muy cómodo en tu casa.
I feel very comfortable in your house.

compañero/-a m./f.   *companion, mate*
Pedro es un buen compañero de viaje.
Peter is a good traveling companion.

compartir   *to share*
¿Podemos compartir la cuenta?
Can we share the bill?

complacido/-a   *pleased*
Estuve muy complacido con la conferencia.
I was very pleased with the conference.

completamente   *completely*
Yo también, completamente complacido.
I was also completely pleased.

compra f.   *purchase*
Hice una buena compra en el mercado.
I made a good purchase at the market.

comprar(se)   *to buy*
¿Dónde puedo comprar artesanías?
Where can I buy handcrafts?

comprender   *to understand*
No te comprendo.
I do not understand you.

computadora (portátil)   *computer, laptop*
Necesito una computadora para conectarme a la red.
I need a computer to connect to the Internet.

común   *common*
El arroz es muy común en la cocina hispánica.
Rice is very common in Hispanic cuisine.

comunicación f.   *communication*
La comunicación es la clave de una buena relación.
Communication is the key to a good relationship.

con (gusto)   *with (pleasure)*
¿Quieres ir al cine con Isabel y conmigo? ¡Con gusto!
Do you want to go to the movies with Isabel and me? With pleasure!

concluir   *to conclude*
Para concluir la visita de la ciudad visitaremos la catedral.
To conclude the city tour we will visit the cathedral.

condición f.   *condition*
No podemos ir en estas condiciones.
We can't go under these conditions.

condón m.   *condom*
Es peligroso tener relaciones sexuales sin condón.
Having sex without a condom is dangerous.

conducir   *to drive, to conduct*
Conduce con cuidado.
Drive carefully.

conectar(se)   *to connect, to get connected*
¿Dónde puedo conectarme a la red?
Where can I connect to the Internet?

conexión (inalámbrica) f.   *(wireless) connection*
¿Hay una conexión inalámbrica en la habitación?
Is there a wireless connection in the room?

confirmar   *to confirm*
Debes de confirmar tu reservación antes de tu vuelo.
You must confirm your reservation before your flight.

conmigo   *with me*
¿Estás conmigo o en contra mía?
Are you with me or against me?

conocer   *to meet, to know*
Tengo mucho gusto en conocerte.
I am very pleased to meet you.

conocido/-a   *well-known*
Frida Kahlo es una conocida pintora mexicana.
Frida Kahlo is a well-known Mexican painter.

conseguir   *to obtain / to achieve*
Consiguió una beca para estudiar en Perú.
He obtained a scholarship to study in Peru.

consejo m.   *advice*
Toma mi consejo.
Take my advice.

considerado/-a   *considerate*
Francisco es una persona muy considerada.
Francisco is a very considerate person.

construir   *to build*
Están construyendo un nuevo centro comercial en las afueras de
la ciudad.
They are building a new mall on the outskirts of the city.

consulado m.   *consulate*
Debo averiguar la dirección del consulado.
I must find out the consulate's address.

consultar   *to consult*
¿Necesitas consultar a un médico?
Do you need to consult a doctor?

contar   *to count, to tell*
Te voy a contar un cuento.
I am going to tell you a story.

contener   *to contain/to hold*
Los bomberos pudieron contener el fuego.
The firemen were able to contain the fire.

contento/-a   *happy*
Estoy muy contento.
I am very happy.

contestar   *to answer, to reply*
Contesta el teléfono por favor.
Answer the telephone, please.

contigo   *with you*
Queremos ir contigo.
We want to go with you.

continuar   *to continue*
Continúa derecho para llegar al museo.
Keep going straight to get to the museum.

contra   *against*
Se tiene que hacer algo contra la adicción a las drogas.
Something must be done against drug addiction.

copia (de seguridad) f.   *copy, backup*
Este no es el original, es una copia.
This is not the original; it's a copy.

copiar   *to copy*
Siempre copio mis archivos por si acaso.
I always copy my files just in case.

correcto/-a   *right, correct*
Estás en lo correcto.
You're right.

correo (aéreo, electrónico) m.   *(air, e-) mail/post office*
¿Me puede decir dónde está el correo?
Can you tell me where the post office is?

correr *to run*
Camina, no corras.
Walk, don't run.

corto/-a *short*
Estos pantalones son demasiado cortos para mí.
These pants are too short for me.

cosa f. *thing*
¿Venden muchas cosas en el mercado de artesanía?
Do they sell many things at the handcraft market?

costar *to cost*
¿Cuánto cuesta este cuadro?
How much is this painting?

costo m. *cost, price*
Su costo es incalculable.
Its price is invaluable.

crear *to create*
Algunas personas crean—-otras solamente copian.
Some people create—-others just copy.

creer *to believe*
Creo que el museo cierra a las cinco.
I believe the museum closes at five.

cuaderno m. *notebook*
Voy a apuntar tu número de teléfono en mi cuaderno.
I am going to write your phone number in my notebook.

cualquier (cosa) *any (thing), whichever*
Podemos ir a verlas cualquier día.
We can go see them any day.

cualquiera *anyone*
No cualquiera puede pintar como Picasso.
Not anyone can paint like Picasso.

cuarto m. *room*
¿Cuánto cuesta la noche en un cuarto doble?
How much is a double room per night?

cubrir(se) *to cover, to cover up*
Puedes cubrirte con esta cobija.
You can cover yourself with this blanket.

cuenta f.   *account, bill (check)*
La cuenta, por favor.
The check, please.

cuento m.   *story*
¿Quieres que te cuente un cuento?
Do you want me to tell you a story?

cuidado m.   *care, be careful!*
Tienes que tener cuidado.
You have to be careful.

cuidar(se)   *to take care, to look after*
¡Adiós! ¡Cuídate mucho!
Good-bye! Take good care of yourself!

cumpleaños m.   *birthday*
¿Cuándo es tu cumpleaños?
When is your birthday?

cuota f.   *fee/quota*
Tienes que pagar una cuota para entrar.
You have to pay a fee to get in.

cura f.   *cure*
Sería magnífico encontrar una cura para el cáncer.
It would be great to find a cure for cancer.

D

dama f.   *lady*
¡Bienvenidos, damas y caballeros!
Welcome, ladies and gentlemen!

dar   *to give*
Silvia le dio un regalo de cumpleaños a Susana.
Silvia gave Susana a birthday present.

datos m. pl.   *data, information*
No tengo muchos datos sobre el asunto.
I don't have much information on the matter.

de   *from, of*
¿De dónde eres?
Where are you from?

debajo (de)   *under, beneath*
El gato está escondido debajo de la mesa.
The cat is hidden under the table.

deber   *must, to owe (money), duty*
Me debes cincuenta dólares y debes pagármelos.
You owe me fifty dollars and you must pay me.

débil   *weak*
Todavía me siento débil después de la enfermedad que tuve.
I still feel weak after the illness I had.

decidir(se)   *to decide*
No tienes que decidirte ahora mismo.
You don't have to decide right now.

decir   *to say, to tell*
Es difícil decir adiós.
It's hard to say good-bye.

declarar   *to declare, to state*
No tengo nada que declarar.
I don't have anything to declare.

dejar   *to leave, to allow, to set down*
¿Puedo dejar esto aquí?
Can I leave this here?

delante (de)   *in front of*
El palacio municipal está delante de la iglesia.
The city hall is in front of the church.

delgado/-a   *thin*
Los españoles se mantienen delgados porque caminan mucho.
Spaniards keep thin because they walk a lot.

delicioso/-a   *delicious*
Este platillo está delicioso.
This dish is delicious.

demasiado/-a   *too much*
No me gusta beber demasiado.
I don't like to drink too much.

demora f.   *delay*
La demora del vuelo es de dos horas.
The flight's delay is two hours.

dentro (de)   *inside*
Todos están dentro de la casa porque hace frío afuera.
Everyone is inside because it's cold outside.

departamento m.   *department, apartment (L. Am.)*
Estoy buscando un departamento que no sea muy caro.
I am looking for an apartment which is not too expensive.

depositar   *to deposit*
Quisiera depositar este dinero en el banco.
I would like to deposit this money in the bank.

deprisa   *quickly*
Hay que terminar deprisa.
We must finish quickly.

derecha f.   *right (direction)*
Da vuelta a la derecha en la próxima esquina.
Turn to the right at the next corner.

derecho   *straight (ahead)*
Si caminas derecho encontrarás la dirección que estás buscando.
If you walk straight ahead you will find the address you are looking for.

desaparecer   *to disappear*
Muchas especies están a punto de desaparecer del planeta.
Many species are about to disappear from the planet.

desayunar   *to eat breakfast*
Vamos a desayunar temprano en la mañana.
We will eat breakfast early in the morning.

descansar   *to rest*
Necesito descansar antes de continuar.
I need to rest before going on.

descanso (tomar un) m.   *rest, break (take a)*
Te recomiendo tomar un descanso por la tarde.
I recommend that you take a break in the afternoon.

descargar   *to download*
No te olvides de descargar tus mensajes en la computadora.
Don't forget to download your messages on your computer.

desconectar   *to disconnect, to unplug*
Desconecta la plancha antes de salir.
Unplug the iron before leaving.

desconocido/-a   *unknown*
No temas a lo desconocido.
Don't fear the unknown.

descontento/-a   *dissatisfied, unhappy*
Mi esposa está descontenta con la habitación del hotel.
My wife is unsatisfied with the hotel room.

describir   *to describe*
Describa lo que quiere comprar.
Describe what you want to buy.

descubrir   *to discover, to uncover*
Cristóbal Colón descubrió América.
Christopher Columbus discovered America.

desde   *since*
Este restaurant ha estado abierto desde 1952.
This restaurant has been open since 1952.

desear   *to desire, to wish, to want*
Deseo tener una casa en la playa.
I wish I had a house on the beach.

desempacar   *to unpack*
Quiero desempacar antes de salir a cenar.
I want to unpack before going out to dinner.

deseo m.   *wish, desire*
Pide un deseo cuando veas la primera estrella.
Make a wish when you see the first star.

desgracia f.   *misfortune*
¡Qué desgracia!
What a misfortune!

despacio   *slowly*
Camine despacio para evitar caerse.
Walk slowly to avoid falling.

desperdiciar   *to waste*
No desperdicies tu energía en cosas vanas.
Don't waste your energy on useless things.

despertador m.   *alarm clock*
No olvides tu despertador porque lo necesitas para llegar a tiempo.
Do not forget your alarm clock because you need it to be on time.

despertar(se)   *to wake up*
No se puede despertar a tiempo sin el despertador.
He can't wake up on time without the alarm clock.

después   *after*
Cenaremos después de ir al cine.
We will have dinner after going to the movies.

destino m.   *destination, destiny*
Espero que llegue bien, cualquiera que sea su destino.
I hope you arrive safely, wherever your destination may be.

detener(se)   *to hold, to stop*
Es muy difícil detener un caballo que corre a toda velocidad.
It's very hard to stop a horse that's running at full speed.

detrás (de)   *behind*
La fuente está en el centro de la plaza.
The fountain is in the middle of the square.

devolver   *to give back*
Le vamos a devolver su dinero.
We will give you back your money.

día (feriado/de fiesta) m.   *day, holiday*
El día de Navidad es un día feriado.
Christmas day is a holiday.

diferente   *different*
Le aseguro que son radicalmente diferentes.
I assure you they are radically different.

difícil   *difficult*
El español no es un idioma difícil de aprender.
Spanish is not a difficult language to learn.

dinero m.   *money*
Necesito cambiar dinero.
I need to exchange money/currency.

dios   *god*
Los aztecas tenían muchos dioses.
The Aztecs had many gods.

dirección f.   *address, direction*
¿Tiene una dirección electrónica?
Do you have an e-mail address?

discriminar   *to discriminate*
Cuando discriminamos atentamos contra los derechos civiles.
When we discriminate we threaten civil rights.

disculpa f.   *apology*
Le debo una disculpa por mi tardanza.
I owe you an apology for my tardiness.

disculpar(se)   *to excuse, to apologize*
Discúlpeme, por favor.
Excuse me, please.

discutir   *to discuss, to argue*
No se debe de levantar la voz al discutir.
One should not raise one's voice when arguing.

disfrutar   *to enjoy*
Disfruté mucho la película.
I really enjoyed the movie.

distancia f.   *distance*
¿Cuál es la distancia entre Madrid y Barcelona?
What's the distance between Madrid and Barcelona?

diversión f.   *entertainment, attraction*
La ciudad ofrece muchas diversiones.
The city offers many attractions.

divertir(se)   *to amuse, to entertain, to have fun*
Nos divertimos mucho anoche.
We had a lot of fun last night.

divisa f.   *foreign currency*
Necesito comprar divisas para mi viaje.
I need to buy foreign currency for my trip.

doblar   *to fold, to turn*
Cuando llegue al final de la calle doble a la izquierda.
When you reach the end of the street turn left.

doble m.   *double*
Estoy dispuesto a pagar el doble y hasta el triple.
I'm willing to pay double and even triple.

documento m.   *document*
No olvides hacer una copia de seguridad de tus documentos.
Don't forget to make a backup copy of your documents.

doloroso/-a   *painful*
Por suerte, la caída no fue muy dolorosa.
Luckily, the fall wasn't very painful.

dormir(se)   *to sleep, to fall asleep*
Ayer nos dormimos antes de las diez.
Yesterday we fell asleep before ten.

dormitorio m.   *bedroom*
La casa tiene dos dormitorios.
The house has two bedrooms.

droga f.   *drug*
Las drogas son ilegales en la mayoría de los países.
Drugs are illegal in most countries.

dudar   *to doubt, to hesitate*
Dudo que este sea el camino correcto.
I doubt that this is the right road.

dulce   *sweet/candy*
Alicia es muy dulce y le gustan mucho los dulces.
Alicia is very sweet and likes candy very much.

durante   *during*
No se pueden usar teléfonos celulares durante el vuelo.
You can't use cell phones during the flight.

durar   *to last*
Esta vela es muy pequeña y no va a durar prendida.
This candle is very short and won't stay lit long.

duro/-a   *hard*
Este pedazo de pan está muy duro.
This piece of bread is very hard.

E

edificio m.   *building*
Los edificios coloniales son muy bellos.
Colonial-style buildings are very beautiful.

educación f.   *education, manners*
La educación se adquiere en la escuela y la buena educación en la casa.
Education is acquired at school and good manners at home.

efectivamente *indeed, really*
Efectivamente, estas ruinas son muy antiguas.
Indeed, these ruins are very ancient.

efectivo/-a *cash/effective*
Pagué con un cheque porque no tenía efectivo.
I paid with a check because I didn't have cash.

ejemplo m. *example*
La catedral es un ejemplo de arquitectura barroca.
The cathedral is an example of baroque architecture.

ejercicio m. *exercise*
El ejercicio físico es indispensable para la buena salud.
Physical exercise is necessary for good health.

elegante *elegant, fancy*
Tengo ganas de ir a cenar a un lugar elegante.
I feel like going to a fancy place for dinner.

elegir *to choose, to elect*
Es difícil elegir un destino sin información.
It is difficult to choose a destination without information.

elevado/-a *high, raised*
Las ruinas de Machu Picchu están en una cima muy elevada.
The ruins of Machu Picchu are on a very high summit.

elevador m. *elevator*
Si hay un terremoto, no tomes el elevador.
If there's an earthquake, don't take the elevator.

embajada f. *embassy*
La embajada está cerca del hotel.
The embassy is near the hotel.

embarazada f. *pregnant*
Creo que estoy embarazada. / Creo que está embarazada.
I think I'm pregnant. / I think she's pregnant.

embarcar(se) *to board*
¿A qué hora debemos embarcar?
At what time should we board?

emergencia f. *emergency*
¡Esto es una emergencia!
This is an emergency!

emocionante   *exciting*
Será un viaje muy emocionante.
It will be a very exciting trip.

empacar   *to pack*
Es necesario empacar con cuidado antes de salir de viaje.
It's necessary to pack carefully before leaving on a trip.

empezar   *to begin, to start*
¿A qué hora empieza el espectáculo?
At what time does the show start?

emplear   *to employ, to use*
Empleo mi computadora todos los días.
I use my computer every day.

empleo m.   *job, employment*
Jorge no ha podido encontrar empleo.
Jorge hasn't been able to find a job.

empresa f.   *business*
La empresa para la que trabajo es muy exitosa.
The business that I work for is very successful.

empujar   *to push*
¡No me empujes!
Don't push me!

en (seguida)   *in, on, at (once)*
El dependiente nos atendió en seguida.
The store clerk assisted us at once.

en vez de   *instead of*
Compraré esta camisa en vez de aquélla.
I will buy this shirt instead of that one.

enamorarse (de)   *to fall in love*
Raquel y Alfonso se enamoraron a primera vista.
Raquel and Alfonso fell in love at first sight.

encender   *to light, to turn on*
¿Puedo encender la luz?
May I turn on the light?

enchufe m.   *electrical outlet/plug*
Necesito un enchufe trifásico para enchufar mi computadora.
I need a grounded, three-pin outlet to plug in my computer.

encima (de)   *on top of*
Coloqué los libros encima de la mesa.
I put the books on top of the table.

encontrar(se)   *to find, to meet*
Podemos encontrarnos en la estación del tren.
We can meet at the train station.

enfrente (de)   *facing, in front of*
La agencia de viajes está enfrente de la oficina de correos.
The travel agency is in front of the post office.

enojar(se)   *to annoy, to anger, to get angry*
Mi hermano se enoja fácilmente.
My brother gets angry easily.

enseñar   *to teach, to show*
El conductor le enseñó su licencia de manejar al policía.
The driver showed the policeman his driver's license.

entender   *to understand*
No entiendo lo que estás diciendo.
I don't understand what you are saying.

entonces   *then*
Entonces, no hay nada que decir.
Then, there is nothing to say.

entrada f.   *entrance, ticket*
Tenemos entradas para ir al cine esta tarde.
We have tickets to go to the cinema this evening.

entrar   *to enter*
Podemos entrar por aquí.
We can enter through here.

entre   *among, between*
Podemos repartir las palomitas entre nosotros.
We can share the popcorn among ourselves.

entregar   *to deliver, to hand over*
Le entregué los documentos al gerente.
I delivered the documents to the manager.

enviar   *to send*
Te enviaré un correo electrónico en cuanto pueda.
I will send you an e-mail as soon as I can.

equipaje m.   *luggage*
Es mejor no llevar mucho equipaje.
It's better not to take a lot of luggage.

equipo m.   *team, equipment*
Para bucear se necesita mucho equipo.
You need a lot of equipment to scuba dive.

equivocado/-a   *wrong*
Me temo que les dieron la información equivocada.
I am afraid they gave you the wrong information.

equivocarse   *to make a mistake*
Se equivocaron de dirección.
They made a mistake on the address.

error m.   *error, mistake*
Claramente hicimos un error al venir aquí.
Clearly we made a mistake coming here.

escalar   *to climb*
Se necesita mucho equipo para escalar una montaña.
You need a lot of equipment to climb a mountain.

escalera f.   *ladder, staircase*
En caso de emergencia use las escalaras.
In case of emergency, use the stairs.

escapar(se)   *to escape*
Todos los huéspedes lograron escapar del incendio.
All the guests managed to escape from the fire.

escoger   *to choose, to select*
No sé qué vestido escoger para el teatro.
I don't know which dress to choose for the theater.

esconder(se)   *to hide*
Los piratas escondieron grandes tesoros en el Caribe.
Pirates hid great treasures in the Caribbean.

escribir   *to write*
Escríbeme seguido, por favor.
Write to me often, please.

escritorio m.   *desk, desktop*
Puse los documentos sobre el escritorio.
I put the documents on the desktop.

escuchar   *to listen*
Escuchar música clásica es uno de mis pasatiempos favoritos.
Listening to classical music is one of my favorite pastimes.

escuela f.   *school*
La escuela está cerrada los fines de semana.
The school is closed on weekends.

ese/esa/esos/esas   *that, those*
Sí, pero no esa.
Yes, but not that one.

esfuerzo m.   *effort*
El esfuerzo trae recompensas.
The effort brings rewards.

eso   *that*
¿Qué es eso?
What is that?

espacio m.   *space*
No hay suficiente espacio en mi maleta para todos los regalos.
There isn't enough space in my suitcase for all the presents.

espacioso/-a   *roomy, spacious*
Necesito una más espaciosa.
I need a more spacious one.

español   *Spanish*
Es útil saber español.
It's useful to know Spanish. Knowing Spanish is useful.

espantar(se)   *to frighten, to get scared*
¡Me espantaste!
You scared me!

especial   *special*
Este ha sido un viaje muy especial para mí.
This has been a very special trip for me.

especialmente   *especially*
Venimos especialmente a verlos.
We came especially to see you.

espejo m.   *mirror*
Deberías verte en el espejo.
You should look at yourself in the mirror.

esperanza f.   *hope*
Nunca se debe de perder la esperanza.
One should never lose hope.

esperar   *to hope, to wait, to expect*
Te voy a esperar enfrente de la iglesia.
I will wait for you in front of the church.

esquina f.   *corner*
Te puedo esperar en la esquina de la calle.
I can wait for you at the street corner.

estación (de policía) f.   *(police) station*
La estación de policía está cerca de la estación del trenes.
The police station is near the train station.

estacionamiento m.   *parking lot*
Es más seguro estacionarse en un estacionamiento.
It's safer to park in a parking lot.

estampilla f.   *postage stamp*
¿Cuántas estampillas necesita esta carta?
How many (postage) stamps does this letter need?

estar   *to be (location, state)*
Estoy cansado pero contento de estar aquí.
I am tired but happy to be here.

este/esta/estos/estas este m.   *this, these/east*
Este es el libro que yo estaba buscando. La España está al este de
la costa este de los Estados Unidos.
*This is the book I was looking for. Spain is east of the United States' east
coast.*

estrecho/-a   *narrow*
Las camas en este hotel son muy estrechas.
The beds in this hotel are very narrow.

estudiar   *to study*
Tengo que estudiar para mis exámenes.
I have to study for my exams.

evitar   *to avoid*
Es necesario evitar los riesgos innecesarios.
It's necessary to avoid unnecessary risks.

exactamente   *exactly*
Le dije exactamente lo que estaba pensando.
I told him exactly what I was thinking.

examen (médico) m.   *exam, (medical) examination*
¿Cuando fue su último examen médico?
When was your last (medical) examination?

examinar   *to examine*
El doctor lo puede examinar mañana por la mañana.
The doctor can examine you tomorrow morning.

excelente   *excellent*
La cena estuvo verdaderamente excelente.
Dinner was truly excellent.

exceso (de equipaje) m.   *excess (baggage)*
Me temo que lleva exceso de equipaje.
I'm afraid you are carrying excess baggage.

éxito m.   *success*
La excursión fue un éxito.
The excursion was a success.

experiencia f.   *experience*
No tengo mucha experiencia pero lo intentaré de todos modos.
I don't have much experience but I will try anyway.

explicación f.   *explanation*
Las explicaciones que nos dieron no están claras.
The explanations they gave us aren't clear.

explicar   *to explain*
¿Me lo puede explicar usted otra vez?
Can you explain it to me again?

exterior m.   *outside*
¿Cuál es la temperatura exterior?
What's the outside temperature?

extrañar   *to miss*
Extraño a mis amigos y a mi familia.
I miss my friends and family.

extranjero/-a   *foreign(er)*
Los extranjeros prefieren hospedarse en hoteles céntricos.
Foreigners prefer to stay at centrally located hotels.

extraviado/-a   *lost*
¿Estás extraviado?
Are you lost?

F

fábrica f.   *factory*
Las fábricas suelen estar en las afueras de las ciudades.
Factories are usually on the outskirts of cities.

fácil   *easy*
Afortunadamente, el problema fue muy fácil de resolver.
Fortunately, the problem was very easy to solve.

facilitar   *to facilitate, to provide*
Conozco a alguien que puede facilitarnos la entrada al
  espectáculo.
I know someone who can facilitate our entrance to the show.

factible   *feasible/possible*
Con el equipo adecuado, es factible escalar la montaña.
With the right gear, climbing the mountain is feasible.

falta f.   *lack/mistake*
He cometido una falta imperdonable.
I have made an unforgivable mistake.

familiar   *familiar*
Tu cara me parece familiar.
Your face seems familiar.

famoso/-a   *famous*
Frida Kahlo es una pintora mexicana muy famosa.
Frida Kahlo is a very famous Mexican painter.

fascinante   *fascinating*
Este libro sobre arqueología maya es fascinante.
This book on Mayan archaeology is fascinating.

fatigado/-a   *tired*
Estoy fatigado de visitar museos todo el día.
I am tired from visiting museums all day.

favor m.   *favor*
Tengo que pedirte que me hagas un favor.
I need to ask you to do me a favor.

favorito/-a   *favorite*
¿Cuál es tu película favorita?
What's your favorite movie?

fecha f.   *date*
¿Cuál es la fecha de hoy?
What's today's date?

felicidad f.   *happiness*
Todos estamos en busca de la felicidad.
We are all in search of happiness.

felicitaciones f. pl.   *congratulations*
Felicitaciones por el premio que ganaste.
Congratulations on the prize you won.

feliz   *happy*
Estoy feliz de estar aquí contigo.
I am happy to be here with you.

feo/-a   *ugly*
Algunos piensan que el arte moderno es feo.
Some people think modern art is ugly.

ferrocarril m.   *railroad*
Es una pena que no haya más ferrocarriles.
It's a pity that there aren't more railroads.

fiesta f.   *party*
Esta tarde hay una fiesta para celebrar el cumpleaños de Rita.
There's a party this afternoon to celebrate Rita's birthday.

fin (de semana) m.   *(week) end*
¿Qué planes tienes para el fin de semana?
What are your plans for the weekend?

final(mente)   *end, final(ly)*
No pudimos quedarnos hasta el final de la película.
We couldn't stay until the end of the movie.

fino/-a   *fine, high quality*
Este encaje hecho a mano es muy fino.
This handmade lace is very high quality.

firma f.   *signature*
Ponga su firma aquí, por favor.
Put your signature here, please.

firmar   *to sign*
Debe de firmar el contrato antes de mudarse al departamento.
You must sign the contract before moving into the apartment.

flaco/-a   *skinny*
Héctor es un muchacho alto y flaco.
Hector is a tall and skinny boy.

flor f.   *flower*
Las rosas son las flores que más me gustan.
Roses are the flowers I like best.

foco (Ec, Méx, Per) m.   *light bulb*
Esta linterna necesita pilas y también un foco nuevo.
This flashlight needs batteries and a new light bulb as well.

fondo m.   *bottom, background*
El tesoro estaba en el fondo del mar.
The treasure was at the bottom of the sea.

fotocopiadora f.   *photocopier/copying machine*
Necesito una fotocopiadora para copiar estas páginas.
I need a photocopier to copy these pages.

fotografía f.   *picture, photography*
Deja que te tome una fotografía.
Let me take your picture.

fracasar   *to fail*
Si lo intentamos seriamente, no fracasaremos.
If we try hard, we won't fail.

franco/-a   *frank, honest*
Un amigo franco es un amigo de verdad.
An honest friend is a true friend.

frecuente(mente)   *frequent(ly)*
Es frecuente encontrar gangas en el mercado.
You can frequently find bargains at the market.

frente f.   *front, forehead*
El frente de esta iglesia está en mal estado.
The front of this church is in bad shape.

frigorífico m.   *refrigerator*
Veamos que podemos encontrar en el frigorífico.
Let's see what we can find in the refrigerator.

frío m.   *cold*
Hoy hace mucho frío.
It's very cold today.

frontera   *border*
Hay muchos problemas en la frontera entre México y los Estados Unidos.
There are many problems at the border between Mexico and the United States.

frotar   *to rub*
Frótate las manos para calentarlas.
Rub your hands to warm them.

fuego m.   *fire*
El fuego consumió el bosque.
Fire burned down the forest.

fuera (de)   *out, outside*
¡Fuera de la casa!
Out of the house!

fuerte   *strong, loud*
No puedo dormir porque la música está muy fuerte.
I can't sleep because the music is very loud.

fuerza f.   *strength*
La unidad hace la fuerza.
There is strength in unity.

fumar   *to smoke*
Ya no se permite fumar en la mayoría de las oficinas.
In most offices smoking is no longer allowed.

funcionar   *to function*
Este radio sólo funciona con pilas.
This radio only functions with batteries.

futuro m.   *future*
¿Qué planes tienes para el futuro?
What plans do you have for the future?

G

gafas f. pl.   *eyeglasses*
No puede ver nada sin sus gafas.
He can't see a thing without his eyeglasses.

ganancia f.   *profit, earnings*
La exportación genera muchas ganancias para el país.
Exports generate a lot of profits for the country.

ganar   *to win, to earn, to gain*
Tomás ganó la carrera fácilmente.
Tomás won the race easily.

gasolina f.   *gasoline*
En España la gasolina se vende por litro.
In Spain gasoline is sold by the liter.

gasolinera f.   *gas station*
Necesitamos encontrar una gasolinera pronto.
We need to find a gas station soon.

gastar   *to spend*
No podemos gastar el dinero en cualquier cosa.
We can't spend money on just anything.

generoso/-a   *generous*
A veces los pobres son más generosos que los ricos.
Sometimes the poor are more generous than the rich.

gente f.   *people*
Este lugar está lleno de gente.
This place is full of people.

gira f.   *tour*
Fuimos de gira por todo el país.
We went on a tour of the whole country.

golpear   *to hit*
A veces la vida golpea muy fuerte.
Sometimes life hits hard.

gordo/-a   *fat, overweight*
No es sano estar gordo.
It's not healthy to be fat.

gozar   *to enjoy*
Mi abuelo ha podido gozar su retiro en buena salud.
My grandfather has been able to enjoy his retirement in good health.

gracias f. pl.   *thank you*
Gracias por su generosa ayuda.
Thank you for your generous help.

gracioso/-a   *graceful/funny*
Se necesita ser gracioso para bailar tango.
One needs to be graceful to dance the tango.

gran, grande   *big, large, great*
Su vecino tiene una casa grande pero un jardín pequeño.
His neighbor has a large house but a small garden.

gratis   *free (cost)*
Las mejores cosas en la vida son gratis.
The best things in life are free.

gratuito/-a   *free (cost), gratuitous*
Los jueves la entrada al museo es gratuita.
On Thursdays, entrance to the museum is free.

grave   *serious*
Espero que no sea nada grave.
I hope it's nothing serious.

gritar   *to shout, to scream*
No necesitas gritar.
You don't need to shout.

grupo m.   *group*
Hay diez personas en nuestro grupo.
There are ten people in our group.

guapo/-a   *handsome*
Martín es un hombre muy guapo.
Martín is a very handsome man.

guardar   *to guard, to keep, to put away*
Deberías guardar el dinero en una caja de seguridad.
You should keep the money in a safe-deposit box.

guerra f.   *war*
Nadie gana en una guerra.
In a war, nobody wins.

guiar   *to guide*
¿Alguien nos puede guiar por el museo?
Can someone guide us through the museum?

gustar   *to like*
Me gusta mucho la comida mexicana.
I like Mexican cooking a lot.

gusto m.   *taste, pleasure*
Mucho gusto en conocerlo.
It's a pleasure to meet you.

H

habitación (doble) f.   *(double) room*
¿Tiene una habitación doble para dos noches?
Do you have a double room for two nights?

hablar   *to talk, to speak*
Quiero aprender a hablar español.
I want to learn how to speak Spanish.

hacer   *to do, to make*
¿Qué vas a hacer esta noche?
What are you doing tonight?

hallar   *to find*
Tenemos que hallar el camino al hotel antes de que anochezca.
We have to find the way to the hotel before it gets dark.

hambre f.   *hunger*
No tengo mucha hambre todavía.
I am not very hungry yet.

hasta   *until*
Te esperé hasta las ocho de la noche.
I waited for you until eight o'clock at night.

hay   *there is, there are*
Hay poco tiempo pero hay muchas cosas que hacer.
There is little time but there are a lot of things to do.

hecho/-a   *done, made*
Estas artesanías están hechas a mano.
These crafts are made by hand.

hermoso/-a   *beautiful*
¡Qué lugar tan hermoso!
What a beautiful place!

hielo m.   *ice*
Un vaso de agua sin hielo, por favor.
A glass of water without ice, please.

historia f.   *history/story*
España es un país con mucha historia.
Spain is a country with a lot of history.

hogar m.   *home*
Es agradable regresar al hogar después de un viaje largo.
It's nice to return home after a long trip.

hola   *hello*
Dile hola a tu hermano de mi parte.
Say hello to your brother on my behalf.

hombre m.   *man*
Andrés es un hombre amable y generoso.
Andrés is a kind and generous man.

hondo/-a   *deep*
¿Qué tan honda es la piscina?
How deep is the pool?

honor m.   *honor*
Antiguamente, las cuestiones de honor se resolvían con sangre.
In olden times, matters of honor were resolved with blood.

honrado/-a   *honest*
Los políticos deberían ser honrados.
Politicians should be honest.

horario m.   *schedule*
¿Dónde puedo consultar el horario de los trenes?
Where can I check the train schedule?

huésped m. & f.   *guest*
Usted es nuestro huésped de honor.
You are our honored guest.

huir   *to flee, to run away*
Los valientes no huyen ante el peligro.
The brave don't run away in the face of danger.

I

idea f.   *idea*
Se me acaba de ocurrir una idea genial.
I just had a great idea.

identificación f. *ID/ identification*
Se necesita identificación para poder entrar al club nocturno.
You need ID to get into the nightclub.

idioma m. *language*
Me encanta aprender nuevos idiomas.
I really like learning new languages.

iglesia f. *church*
Esta iglesia data del siglo dieciséis.
This church dates from the sixteenth century.

igual(mente) *same, likewise*
La comida mexicana en los EE.UU. no es igual a la comida en México.
Mexican food in the U.S. is not the same as food in Mexico.

imaginar *to imagine*
Imagínate las consecuencias.
Imagine the consequences.

importante *important*
Es importante hacer caso de las señales de tráfico.
It's important to pay attention to traffic signs.

imposible *impossible*
Me temo que es imposible hacer lo que me pides.
I'm afraid that what you're asking me to do is impossible.

impresora (de tinta) f. *(ink jet) printer*
Necesito una impresora para imprimir mi pase de abordar.
I need a printer to print my boarding pass.

impuesto m. *tax*
En el aeropuerto venden productos libres de impuestos.
Duty-free products are sold at the airport.

incierto/-a *uncertain*
Los resultados de las elecciones son inciertos todavía.
The election results are still uncertain.

incluir *to include*
No olvides incluir aspirinas en tu botiquín de primeros auxilios.
Don't forget to include aspirin in your first-aid kit.

incómodo/-a *uncomfortable*
Viajar en avión puede ser muy incómodo.
Air travel can be very uncomfortable.

indicar   *to indicate, to tell*
¿Puede indicarme cuál es el tren a Toledo?
Can you tell me which train goes to Toledo?

indispensable   *necessary*
No es indispensable tener mucho dinero para viajar.
It isn't necessary to have a lot of money to travel.

infeliz   *unhappy*
Tu partida me hace muy infeliz.
Your departure makes me very unhappy.

información f.   *information*
Necesitamos más información antes de tomar una decisión.
We need more information before making a decision.

informar   *to inform*
Nos acaban de informar que el vuelo está cancelado.
They just informed us that the flight is cancelled.

informática f.   *information technology*
César sabe mucho de informática.
César knows a lot about information technology.

ingresos m. pl.   *income*
Este año la compañía espera recibir mayores ingresos.
The company expects to receive more income this year.

iniciar   *to begin, to initiate*
No inicies algo que no vas a terminar.
Don't begin something you won't finish.

injusto/-a   *unfair, unjustified*
La vida puede parecer injusta a veces.
Life can seem unfair sometimes.

inmediatamente   *immediately*
Si queremos llegar a tiempo debemos salir inmediatamente.
If we want to be on time we must leave immediately.

inmigración f.   *immigration*
La inmigración ilegal es en parte un resultado de la pobreza.
Illegal immigration is in part the result of poverty.

inocente   *innocent*
Juro que soy inocente.
I swear I'm innocent.

inodoro f.   *toilet*
El inodoro está al fondo a la derecha.
The toilet is in the back to the right.

insatisfecho/-a   *dissatisfied*
Estoy insatisfecho con el servicio en este hotel.
I'm dissatisfied with the service at this hotel.

inspector(a) (de aduanas) m./f.   *inspector, customs officer*
Los inspectores de aduanas en la frontera son muy estrictos.
Customs officers at the border are very strict.

inteligente   *intelligent*
Una persona inteligente sabe cuando cambiar de rumbo.
An intelligent person knows when to change course.

interconexión (de redes) f.   *network*
La interconexión de redes crece más y más rápido cada día.
The network grows bigger and faster every day.

interesante   *interesting*
Ahora mismo hay exposiciones realmente interesantes.
Right now there are really interesting exhibitions.

intérprete m. & f.   *interpreter*
Con este libro, no necesitamos un intérprete.
With this book, we don't need an interpreter.

ir(se)   *to go, to leave*
Es hora de ir a la fiesta, vámonos.
It's time to go to the party, let's go.

izquierda f.   *left*
Si miran a la izquierda verán la Puerta del Sol.
If you look to the left you will see the Puerta del Sol.

J

jabón m.   *soap*
No hay jabón en el baño.
There is no soap in the bathroom.

jalar (L.Am.)   *to pull*
Es más fácil jalar las maletas que cargarlas.
It's easier to pull luggage than to carry it.

jamás   *never*
Jamás había visto algo así.
I had never seen anything like this.

jardín m.   *garden*
¿Te gustaría visitar el jardín botánico?
Would you like to visit the botanical garden?

jefe/-a m./f.   *boss*
Claudia tiene suerte de tener un jefe tan bueno.
Claudia is lucky to have such a good boss.

joven m. & f.   *young*
Además es muy joven.
Besides, he's very young.

juego m.   *game*
Los juegos tradicionales están desapareciendo por los
   videojuegos.
Traditional games are disappearing because of video games.

juez m. & f.   *judge*
Un juez tiene que ser justo y objetivo.
A judge has to be fair and objective.

jugar   *to play (games, sports)*
¿Quieres jugar futbol en el parque?
Do you want to play soccer at the park?

juguete m.   *toy*
Los juguetes hechos a mano son generalmente más bonitos.
Handmade toys are generally prettier.

junto/-a(s)   *next (to), together*
Queremos sentarnos todos juntos.
All of us want to sit together.

justo   *fair*
¡Esto no es justo!
This isn't fair!

juventud f.   *youth*
Uno a veces no aprecia la juventud hasta que llega a viejo.
Sometimes one does not appreciate youth until one becomes old.

K

kilómetro m.   *kilometer*
Una milla equivale aproximadamente a tres kilómetros.
A mile is equivalent to approximately three kilometers.

L

lado m.   *side*
Me gusta caminar a tu lado.
I like to walk by your side.

ladrón(a) m./f.   *thief*
La policía atrapó al ladrón.
The police caught the thief.

lago m.   *lake*
Está prohibido pescar en el lago.
It's forbidden to fish in the lake.

largo/-a   *long*
Necesitas una cuerda más larga para escalar la montaña.
You need a longer rope to climb the mountain.

lata   *(tin) can*
La sopa fresca es mejor que la sopa de lata.
Fresh soup is better than soup from a can.

lavar(se)   *to wash (oneself)*
Lavarse las manos antes de comer es importante.
It's important to wash one's hands before eating.

lección f.   *lesson*
El fracaso enseña una valiosa lección.
Failure teaches a valuable lesson.

leer   *to read*
A mí me encanta leer libros de viaje.
I really like reading travel books.

legal(mente)   *legal(ly)*
No se puede trabajar legalmente sin una visa de trabajo.
You can't work legally without a work visa.

lejano/-a   *distant*
Me gusta viajar a lugares lejanos.
I like to travel to distant places.

lejos (de)   *far (from)*
¿Qué tan lejos está Toledo de Madrid?
How far is Toledo from Madrid?

lenguaje m.   *language*
Los animales tienen sus propios lenguajes.
Animals have their own languages.

lentamente   *slowly*
El tiempo parece pasar más lentamente cerca del mar.
Time seems to pass more slowly by the sea.

lentes m. pl.   *eyeglasses, lenses*
Mi madre necesita lentes para leer.
My mother needs eyeglasses to read.

lento/-a   *slow*
Un tren es más lento que un avión pero más cómodo.
A train is slower than a plane but more comfortable.

letra f.   *letter (alphabet)*
Las primeras letras del alfabeto son a, b y c.
The first letters of the alphabet are a, b, and c.

letrero m.   *(posted) sign*
El letrero indica por dónde ir.
The sign indicates which way to go.

levantar(se)   *to raise, to lift, to get up (out of bed)*
Levantarse temprano y levantar pesas levanta el ánimo.
Getting up early and lifting weights raises the spirit.

ley f.   *law*
Las leyes deben ser obedecidas.
Laws must be obeyed.

liberar   *to free, to liberate*
La verdad libera al hombre.
Truth frees man.

libro m.   *book*
Un buen libro puede ser el mejor compañero de viaje.
A good book can be the best travel companion.

licencia (de conducir) f.   *(driver's) license*
Mi licencia de conducir caducó hace un mes.
My driver's license expired a month ago.

limpiar   *to clean*
¿Puedo pasar a limpiar la habitación?
May I come in to clean the room?

limpio/-a   *clean*
Mantener las manos limpias es muy importante.
It's very important to keep your hands clean.

lindo/-a   *pretty*
Qué lindo vestido. ¿Cuánto cuesta?
What a pretty dress. How much is it?

línea f.   *line*
Traté de llamarte pero la línea telefónica estaba ocupada.
I tried to call you but the telephone line was busy.

liso/-a   *smooth*
Carla tiene el pelo muy liso.
Carla has very smooth hair.

lista f.   *list*
La lista de invitados está muy larga
The guest list is very long.

llamada f.   *call*
Las llamadas de larga distancia pueden ser caras.
Long distance calls can be expensive.

llamar(se)   *to call, to be called*
Se llama María, llámala por teléfono.
Her name is María, call her on the phone.

llave f.   *key*
Te daré una copia de la llave de la casa.
I'll give you a copy of the house key.

llegada f.   *arrival*
¿Cuál es nuestra hora estimada de llegada?
What's our estimated time of arrival?

llegar   *to arrive*
El vuelo llegó a tiempo.
The flight arrived on time.

llenar *to fill*
Es mejor llenar las formas migratorias en el avión.
It's better to fill out the immigration forms on the airplane.

lleno/-a *full*
El vuelo ya está lleno.
The flight is already full.

llevar *to take, to carry*
¿Podemos pedir comida para llevar?
Can we get take-out food?

llorar *to cry*
No llores, todo saldrá bien.
Don't cry; everything will turn out fine.

llover *to rain*
¿Cree que va a llover?
Do you think it's going to rain?

localizar *to locate*
Estoy tratando de localizar un buen hotel.
I'm trying to locate a good hotel.

loco/-a *crazy*
¿Estás loco?
Are you crazy?

luego *later, afterward, then*
Luego de la siesta, podemos salir a pasear.
After our nap, we can go for a stroll.

lugar m. *place*
¿Conoces un buen lugar para comer?
Do you know a good place to eat?

lujo m. *luxury*
Viajar es un lujo necesario.
Traveling is a necessary luxury.

luz f. *light*
La luz de la mañana es la mejor para tomar fotos.
The morning light is the best for taking pictures.

M

madera f.   *wood (material)*
Los juguetes de madera son más caros.
Wooden toys are more expensive.

magnífico/-a   *magnificent*
Las pirámides de México son magníficas.
Mexico's pyramids are magnificent.

mal   *bad(ly), ill*
¿Te sientes mal?
Do you feel ill?

maleta f.   *suitcase*
Mi maleta está llena de regalos para mi familia.
My suitcase is full of presents for my family.

malo/-a   *bad, evil*
Es malo ser una persona mala.
Being an evil person is bad.

malsano/-a   *unhealthy*
La contaminación crea un ambiente malsano.
Pollution creates an unhealthy environment.

mandar   *to send, to order*
Te mandé un correo electrónico, ¿lo recibiste?
I sent you an e-mail, did you get it?

manera f.   *manner, way*
¿Cuál es la mejor manera de llegar al museo?
What's the best way to get to the museum?

mantener   *to keep, to maintain*
Hay que mantener sano el medio ambiente.
We must keep the environment healthy.

mapa f.   *map*
Un buen mapa es imprescindible para el viajero precavido.
A good map is necessary for the cautious traveler.

máquina f.   *machine*
¿Cómo funciona esta máquina?
How does this machine work?

mar m.   *sea*
Me gustaría vivir cerca del mar.
I would like to live by the sea.

maravilloso/-a   *wonderful*
Es un mundo tan maravilloso.
It's a wonderful world.

más (que)   *more (than)*
La amistad vale más que el dinero.
Friendship is worth more than money.

más tarde   *later*
Nos vemos más tarde.
See you later.

matrimonio m.   *marriage*
En teoría, el matrimonio es para siempre.
In theory, marriage is forever.

mayor   *older, greater*
La gente mayor merece respeto.
Older people deserve respect.

medio/-a   *half*
Tengo mucha hambre: me podría comer media docena de
   huevos.
I'm very hungry: I could eat a half-dozen eggs.

medir   *to measure*
La calidad no siempre se puede medir por el precio.
Quality can't always be measured by price.

mejor   *better*
Es mejor viajar en temporada baja.
It's better to travel in the off-season.

mejorar(se)   *to improve, to get better*
Espero que pronto mejore tu situación.
I hope that your situation improves soon.

menor   *younger, smaller*
Ernesto tiene un hermano menor y otro mayor.
Ernesto has one younger brother and one older.

menos (de, que)   *less (than)*
Quiero gastar menos de cien dólares en regalos.
I want to spend less than a hundred dollars on gifts.

mensaje (de texto) m.   *(text) message*
¿Recibiste mi mensaje?
Did you get my message?

mentir   *to lie, to deceive*
¡No me mientas!
Don't lie to me!

mentira f.   *lie*
No hay mentiras pequeñas.
There are no small lies.

menú m,   *menu*
¿Nos puede traer el menú por favor?
Can you bring us the menu please?

mercado (de valores) m.   *(stock) market*
¿Quieres ir al mercado de artesanías?
Do you want to go to the craft market?

mesa f.   *table*
Sentémonos a la mesa para cenar.
Let's sit at the table for dinner.

mesero/-a m./f.   *waiter*
El mesero sirvió la cena.
The waiter served dinner.

metro m.   *subway*
Se puede llegar al aeropuerto en metro.
You can get to the airport on the subway.

mezclar   *to mix*
Mezclar los negocios con el placer puede ser riesgoso.
Mixing business and pleasure can be risky.

microondas m.   *microwave*
Nunca pongas metales en el microondas.
Never put metal in the microwave.

miedo m.   *fear*
Nunca hay que mostrar el miedo.
You must never show fear.

mientras   *(mean)while*
¿Qué podemos hacer mientras esperamos?
What can we do while we wait?

milla f.   *mile*
Una milla equivale a tres kilómetros, más o menos.
One mile is the equivalent of three kilometers, more or less.

minus-válido/-a   (adj. and noun) *handicapped*
¿Es accesible para los minusválidos este hotel?
Is this hotel accessible for the handicapped?

minuto m.   *minute*
Puedo estar listo en cinco minutos.
I can be ready in five minutes.

mirar   *to look (at)*
Es muy relajante mirar el mar.
Watching the sea is very relaxing.

mismo/-a   *same*
Nos quedamos en el mismo hotel que ustedes.
We stayed at the same hotel you did.

mitad f.   *half*
Si quieres, puedo pagar la mitad de la cuenta.
If you want, I can pay half of the bill.

moderado/-a   *moderate*
Es más seguro conducir a una velocidad moderada.
It's safer to drive at a moderate speed.

modo m.   *way, manner*
Le gusta hacer las cosas a su modo.
He likes to do things his way.

mojado/-a   *wet*
Ten cuidado: el piso está mojado.
Be careful: the floor is wet.

molestar   *to bother, to annoy*
Me molesta la gente grosera.
Rude people annoy me.

momento m.   *moment*
¿Me puedes esperar un momento aquí?
Can you wait here for me a moment?

moneda f.   *coin, currency*
¿Cómo se llama la moneda peruana?
What's the Peruvian currency called?

montaña f.   *mountain*
El Aconcagua es la montaña más alta de las Américas.
Aconcagua is the tallest mountain in the Americas.

moreno/-a   *dark-haired/dark-skinned*
Las personas morenas son menos propensas a las quemaduras de
   sol.
Dark-skinned people are less prone to sunburn.

morir   *to die*
¿Vale la pena morir por una idea?
Is it worth dying for an idea?

mostrar   *to show*
¿Quiere que le muestre algo?
Would you like me to show you something?

mover(se)   *to move, to displace*
¡No te muevas!
Don't move!

muchacha f.   *young girl/maid*
Esa muchacha se llama Marta.
That girl's name is Marta.

muchacho m.   *young man*
Aquel muchacho es Miguel, su novio.
That young man over there is Miguel, her boyfriend.

muchas veces   *many times*
¿Has viajado muchas veces en tren?
Have you traveled on a train many times?

mucho (gusto)   *much/(pleased to meet you)*
No nos queda mucho tiempo.
We don't have much time left.

muerto/-a   *dead*
En México se celebra el Día de Muertos.
In Mexico, they celebrate the Day of the Dead.

mujer f.   *woman*
Eva fue la primera mujer según la Biblia.
Eve was the first woman according to the Bible.

multa f.   *fine, ticket*
Maneja despacio si no quieres recibir una multa.
Drive slowly if you don't want to get a ticket.

mundo m.   *world*
El mundo es muy pequeño.
The world is very small.

muñeca f.   *doll*
Vi unas muñecas hechas a mano en el mercado.
I saw some handmade dolls at the market.

museo m.   *museum*
El museo de arte moderno es muy interesante.
The modern art museum is very interesting.

música f.   *music*
La música es un lenguaje universal.
Music is a universal language.

muy (bien)   *very (well)*
Estoy muy bien, gracias.
I'm very well, thank you.

N

nacer   *to be born*
¿En qué día naciste?
On what day were you born?

nacionalidad f.   *nationality/citizenship*
Los puertorriqueños tienen nacionalidad estadounidense.
Puerto Ricans have U.S. citizenship.

nada   *nothing*
No hay nada que hacer.
There is nothing to do.

nadar   *to swim*
Nadar de noche en el mar es peligroso.
Swimming in the sea at night is dangerous.

nadie   *nobody*
Nadie aquí sabe inglés.
Nobody here knows English.

Navidad f.   *Christmas*
Te deseo una feliz Navidad.
I wish you a Merry Christmas.

necesario/-a   *necessary*
Es necesario tener una reservación.
It is necessary to have a reservation.

necesitar   *to need*
¿Necesitas ayuda?
Do you need help?

negar(se)   *to deny/to refuse*
Si lo sabes, no lo niegues.
If you know it, don't deny it.

nieve f.   *snow*
En el trópico sólo hay nieve en las montañas.
In the tropics there's only snow in the mountains.

ningún, ninguno/-a   *none*
Ninguno de nosotros sabe dónde estamos.
None of us knows where we are.

niño/-a m./f.   *child*
Este niño es hijo de Víctor.
This child is Víctor's son.

nombre m.   *name*
¿Cuál es tu nombre?
What's your name?

norte m.   *north*
Para evitar perderse hay que saber dónde está el norte.
To avoid getting lost you must know where north is.

notar   *to notice*
No noté la señal de desviación y me perdí.
I didn't notice the detour sign and I got lost.

novio/-a m./f.   *groom/bride, boy/girlfriend*
La novia y el novio se van a casar.
The bride and the groom are going to be married.

nuevamente   *again*
Intentemos nuevamente.
Let's try again.

nuevo/-a   *new*
Esta nueva edición es mejor que la anterior.
This new edition is better than the previous one.

nunca   *never*
    Es mejor tarde que nunca.
    It's better late than never.

O

o   *or, either*
    ¿Vienes o te quedas?
    Are you coming or staying?

objeto m.   *object*
    Los objetos prehispánicos son muy valiosos.
    Pre-hispanic objects are very valuable.

obra f.   *work*
    Esta pintura es una obra de arte.
    This painting is a work of art.

obtener   *to get, to obtain*
    Tienes que trabajar duro para obtener lo que quieres.
    You have to work hard to get what you want.

océano m.   *ocean*
    El Canal de Panamá conecta el océano Atlántico con el Pacífico.
    The Panama Canal connects the Atlantic Ocean with the Pacific.

ocupado/-a   *busy*
    Joaquín siempre está ocupado.
    Joaquín is always busy.

odiar   *to hate*
    Odia su trabajo.
    He hates his job.

oeste m.   *west*
    Cristóbal Colón quería llegar a la India navegando hacia el oeste.
    Christopher Columbus wanted to reach India by sailing west.

oficina f.   *office*
    Tiene que ir a la oficina todos los días.
    He has to go to the office every day.

ofrecer   *to offer*
    ¿Puedo ofrecerle algo de beber?
    Can I offer you something to drink?

oír *to hear*
¿Oyes esa música?
Do you hear that music?

oler *to smell*
La comida huele bien.
The food smells good.

olor m. *smell*
Aquí adentro hay un olor extraño.
There's a strange smell in here.

olvidar *to forget*
No olvides la llave de casa.
Don't forget the house key.

oportunidad f. *chance, opportunity*
Necesito otra oportunidad para probar que puedo hacerlo.
I need another chance to prove I can do it.

ordenador m. *computer (Sp.)*
Los ordenadores se han vuelto indispensables.
Computers have become indispensable.

ordenar *to (put in) order, to command*
Estamos listos para ordenar la cena.
We are ready to order dinner.

organizar(se) *to organize, to get organized*
Los obreros organizaron una gran manifestación.
The workers organized a big protest.

oro m. *gold*
No todo lo que brilla es oro.
Not all that glitters is gold.

oscuro/-a *dark*
En una noche oscura las estrellas brillan más.
The stars shine brighter on a dark night.

otra vez *again*
Queremos pasar el día en la playa otra vez.
We want to spend the day at the beach again.

otro/-a *another*
Necesito que me des otra oportunidad.
I need you to give me a second chance.

P

pagar   *to pay*
¿Puedo pagar con mi tarjeta de crédito?
Can I pay with my credit card?

página (electrónica) f.   *(web) page*
Tengo una página electrónica personal.
I have a personal web page.

pago m.   *payment*
El pago de la renta se debe hacer en el banco.
The rent payment must be made at the bank.

país m.   *country*
¿Cuántos países has visitado?
How many countries have you visited?

palabra f.   *word*
Estas son las palabras más útiles en español.
These are the most useful words in Spanish.

papel (higiénico) m.   *(toilet) paper*
Necesitamos comprar papel higiénico.
We need to buy toilet paper.

paquete m.   *package*
¿Dónde puedo enviar este paquete?
Where can I mail this package?

para   *for (recipient, purpose), to (direction/destination), in order to, by (deadline)*
El regalo para mi mamá estará listo para mañana.
The present for my mom will be ready by tomorrow.

parada (de autobús) f.   *(bus) stop*
La parada de autobús está en la esquina de la calle.
The bus stop is at the corner of the street.

paraguas m.   *umbrella*
¿Crees que debamos llevar un paraguas?
Do you think we should take an umbrella?

parar(se)   *to stop, to stand up*
El autobús para en la esquina.
The bus stops at the corner.

parecer(se) *to appear, to seem, to look like*
Parece que va a llover.
It looks like it's going to rain.

parte f. *part*
¿De qué parte de Chile eres?
What part of Chile are you from?

partido (político) m. *match (sport), political party*
Vimos el partido de futbol en la televisión.
We watched the soccer match on T.V.

partir *to depart/to split*
Ha llegado la hora de que partamos.
The time has come for us to depart.

pasado (mañana) m. *past, (day after tomorrow)*
Salimos para Ecuador pasado mañana.
We leave for Ecuador the day after tomorrow.

pasaje m. *passage, ticket*
El pasaje de avión fue muy caro.
The plane ticket was very expensive.

pasajero/-a m./f. *passenger*
El pasajero perdió el avión.
The passenger missed the plane.

pasaporte m. *passport*
Se necesita un pasaporte válido para viajar.
You need a valid passport to travel.

pasar *to pass, to enter, to happen*
¿Qué pasó anoche?
What happened last night?

pase m. *pass, permit*
Es muy conveniente poder imprimir los pases de abordar en casa.
It's very convenient to be able to print the boarding passes at home.

pasear *to take a walk*
¿Quieres ir a pasear por el parque?
Do you want to take a walk in the park?

pastilla f. *pill, tablet*
Las pastillas para dormir pueden ser adictivas.
Sleeping pills can be addictive.

paz f. *peace*
Todos deseamos que haya paz en el mundo.
We all wish for peace on earth.

peatón m. & f. *pedestrian*
En las ciudades grandes los peatones no tienen prioridad.
In big cities pedestrians don't have priority.

pedazo m. *piece*
¿Me pasas un pedazo de pan?
Can you pass me a piece of bread?

pedir *to ask for, to request*
Te tengo que pedir un favor.
I have to ask you for a favor.

pelea f. *fight*
No estoy buscando una pelea.
I'm not looking for a fight.

película f. *movie, film*
¿Has visto esa película?
Have you seen that movie?

peligro m. *danger*
Muchas especies están en peligro de extinción.
Many species are in danger of extinction.

peligroso/-a *dangerous*
Manejar a alta velocidad es peligroso.
Driving at high speeds is dangerous.

pelota f. *ball*
Aviéntame la pelota
Throw me the ball.

pensar *to think*
¿En qué piensas?
What are you thinking about?

peor *worse*
Hoy me siento peor que ayer.
Today I feel worse than yesterday.

pequeño/-a *small, short*
Tomemos un pequeño descanso.
Let's take a short break.

perder(se)   *to lose, to miss (a flight), to get lost*
Es fácil perderse en esta ciudad.
It's easy to get lost in this city.

pérdida f.   *loss*
No podemos remediar la pérdida de su equipaje.
We can't remedy the loss of his luggage.

perdonar   *to forgive, to excuse*
Es más fácil perdonar que olvidar.
It's easier to forgive than to forget.

perfecto/-a   *perfect*
Encontré el regalo perfecto en la feria de artesanías.
I found the perfect gift at the craft fair.

periódico m.   *newspaper*
Yo recibo el periódico todos los días.
I receive the newspaper every day.

permiso (de conducir) m.   *permission, driving permit*
No necesitas mi permiso para salir.
You don't need my permission to go out.

permitir   *to allow*
¿Se permite fumar aquí?
Is smoking allowed here?

pero   *but*
Fuimos al museo pero estaba cerrado.
We went to the museum but it was closed.

perseguir   *to pursue, to chase*
El perro me persiguió hasta la casa.
The dog chased me all the way home.

pesado/-a   *heavy*
El paquete está muy pesado.
The package is very heavy.

peso m.   *weight*
¿Se vende por peso o por pieza?
Do you sell it by weight or by count?

piel f.   *skin/leather, fur*
No necesitarás tu abrigo de piel en Cancún.
You won't need your fur coat in Cancún.

pila f.   *battery*
¿Qué tipo de pilas necesita tu linterna?
What kind of batteries does your flashlight need?

píldora f.   *pill*
¿Crees que necesitemos píldoras contra la malaria?
Do you think we need anti-malarial pills?

piscina f.   *pool*
Vamos a tomar el sol cerca de la piscina.
Let's go sunbathe by the pool.

piso m.   *floor, apartment (Sp.)*
¿Cuántos pisos tiene este edificio?
How many floors does this building have?

plano/-a m.   *map/ (as adj., flat)*
Pedí un plano del museo.
I asked for a map of the museum.

plato m.   *dish, plate*
Este es un plato de plata de la época colonial.
This is a silver plate from the colonial period.

playa f.   *beach*
¡Vamos a la playa!
Let's go to the beach!

plaza f.   *town square*
La multitud se reunió en la plaza.
The crowd gathered in the town square.

pluma f.   *feather/pen*
¿Puede prestarme su pluma?
Can I borrow your pen?

pobre   *poor*
Aquí vive mucha gente pobre.
Many poor people live here.

poco/-a(s)   *little, few*
Existen pocas fuentes de trabajo.
Few sources of employment exist.

poder   *to be able to/ (as masculine noun) power*
No hay nada que podemos hacer.
There is nothing we can do.

policía f./m. & f.   *police/police officer*
Hay que llamar a la policía.
We must call the police.

poner(se)   *to put, to put on*
¿Dónde quieres que ponga esto?
Where do you want me to put this?

por   *for, because of, around, by, through*
Vamos a hacer un viaje por barco por el Caribe.
We're going on a trip around the Caribbean by boat.

por favor   *please*
Tome asiento por favor.
Take a seat please.

por supuesto   *of course*
Por supuesto que me gusta viajar.
Of course I like to travel.

porque   *because*
Vamos porque se hace tarde.
Let's go because it's getting late.

portátil   *portable*
Mi portafolio es una oficina portátil.
My portfolio is a portable office.

posible   *possible*
Creen que es posible mejorar su situación inmigrando.
They believe that it's possible to improve their situation by immigrating.

precio m.   *price*
Me parece que el precio está demasiado alto.
It seems to me that the price is too high.

preferir   *to prefer*
Algunos prefieren ir a la capital; otros al extranjero.
Some prefer to go to the capital; others abroad.

pregunta f.   *question*
Yo tengo una pregunta.
I have a question.

preguntar   *to ask*
No me preguntes por qué.
Don't ask me why.

preocupar(se)   *to worry*
No hay de qué preocuparse.
There's nothing to worry about.

preparar(se)   *to prepare, to get ready*
Lo mejor es prepararse para todo.
The best thing to do is to prepare for anything.

presentar(se)   *to present, to introduce*
Permítame que le presente a mi jefe.
Allow me to introduce you to my boss.

preservativo m.   *condom*
Los preservativos previenen las enfermedades venéreas.
Condoms prevent venereal diseases.

presión f.   *pressure*
Hay mucha presión para reducir el flujo de inmigrantes ilegales.
There is a lot of pressure to reduce the flow of illegal immigrants.

prevenir   *to prevent*
Para prevenir las epidemias hay que mantener estrictas normas de higiene.
To prevent epidemics we have to keep strict hygiene regulations.

primer, primero/-a   *first*
Hoy es el primer día de nuestras vacaciones.
Today is the first day of our vacation.

principal   *main*
¿Cuál es la razón principal de su viaje?
What's the main reason for your trip?

principiar   *to begin, to start*
Lo más difícil es principiar una tarea.
The hardest thing is to begin a chore.

prisa f.   *hurry, rush*
Tengo prisa por llegar a la estación de tren.
I'm in a hurry to get to the train station.

privado/-a   *private*
Sería divertido tener un avión privado.
It would be fun to have a private plane.

problema m.   *problem*
La drogadicción es un problema social.
Drug addiction is a social problem.

procesador de palabras/de textos m.   *word processor*
Ya no puedo imaginar la vida sin los procesadores de palabras.
I can no longer imagine life without word processors.

producir   *to produce*
Las drogas se producen en el sur pero se consumen en el norte.
Drugs are produced in the south but they are consumed in the north.

programa (de computadora) m.   *program/computer software*
Ahora hay programas de computadora para todo.
Now there's computer software for everything.

prometer   *to promise*
Prométeme que regresarás.
Promise me that you will return.

pronto   *soon, quickly*
Pronto estará lista la cena.
Dinner will be ready soon.

propina f.   *tip*
La propina suele ser el quince por ciento.
The tip is usually fifteen percent.

proteger   *to protect*
Hay que proteger el medio ambiente.
We must protect the environment.

próximo/-a   *next*
Nos bajamos en la próxima estación.
We're getting off at the next station.

pueblo m.   *town, village/ people*
Este pueblo es muy pintoresco.
This town is very picturesque.

puente m.   *bridge*
Los incas construían largos puentes de cuerda.
The Incas built long rope bridges.

puerta (principal) f.   *(front) door, gate*
La puerta principal está cerrada.
The front door is closed.

puntual(mente)   *punctual(ly), on time*
Los trenes suelen ser más puntuales que los aviones.
Trains tend to be more punctual than planes.

Q

quedar(se)   *to remain, to stay*
Es mejor quedarnos aquí hasta que pare de llover.
We had better stay here until it stops raining.

queja f.   *complaint*
¿Dónde puedo poner una queja?
Where can I lodge a complaint?

quejarse   *to complain*
No sirve de nada quejarse.
It's no use to complain.

querer   *to want, to love*
Raquel quiere mucho a Carlos.
Raquel loves Carlos very much.

querido/-a   *dear*
Gracias por venir, queridos amigos.
Thank you for coming, dear friends.

quincena f.   *fortnight (two weeks)/salary*
Recibo mi quincena cada quincena.
I get my salary every two weeks.

quitar(se)   *to remove, to get out of the way*
Ayúdame a quitar estas cosas de aquí.
Help get these things out of the way.

quizás   *maybe, perhaps*
Quizás llueva mañana.
Perhaps it will rain tomorrow.

R

rápidamente   *rapidly*
Llegaremos más rápidamente en metro.
We'll get there more rapidly on the subway.

rápido   *fast*
Podemos ir a un lugar de comida rápida.
We can go to a fast-food place.

real   *real/royal*
Realmente quiero visitar el palacio real.
I really want to visit the royal palace.

realista	*realistic*
Los patrones dicen que las demandas de los obreros no son realistas.
The employers say that the workers' demands aren't realistic.

rebaja f.	*discount*
Me hicieron un gran descuento en esta compra.
They gave me a great discount on this purchase.

recargo m.	*surcharge*
Si no pagas puntualmente habrá recargos.
If you do not pay on time there will be surcharges.

recibir	*to receive*
¿Recibiste mi correo electrónico?
Did you receive my e-mail?

recibo m.	*receipt*
Cuando compres algo siempre pide un recibo.
When you buy something always ask for a receipt.

reciclar	*to recycle*
Reciclar es una manera de combatir el calentamiento global.
Recycling is a way to fight global warming.

reciente(mente)	*recent(ly)*
El conflicto entre patrones y obreros no es reciente.
The conflict between employers and workers isn't recent.

recomendar	*to recommend*
¿Me puedes recomendar un restaurante bueno pero barato?
Can you recommend a good but cheap restaurant?

reconocer	*to recognize*
No te reconocí.
I did not recognize you.

recordar	*to remember*
Recordaré este viaje por siempre.
I will remember this trip forever.

recto/-a	*straight (ahead)*
Si caminas recto llegarás a la plaza.
If you walk straight ahead you will get to the square.

recuerdo m.	*memory, souvenir*
Tengo agradables recuerdos de mi último viaje a Honduras.
I have nice memories of my last trip to Honduras.

redondo/-a   *round*
Es más barato un viaje redondo que uno sencillo.
A round-trip ticket is cheaper than a one-way one.

reemplazar   *to replace*
Es hora de reemplazar estas pilas.
It's time to replace these batteries.

reflejar(se)   *to reflect, to be reflected*
Se dice que los ojos reflejan el alma de una persona.
It's said that the eyes reflect the soul of a person.

regalo m.   *gift*
Quiero com-prar un regalo para mi madre.
I want to buy a gift for my mother.

regatear   *to bargain*
No me gusta regatear.
I do not like to bargain.

regresar   *to return*
Regresaré a Europa algún día.
I will return to Europe some day.

rehusar   *to refuse*
Me rehúso a pagar los recargos.
I refuse to pay the surcharges.

reina f.   *queen*
La reina es la esposa del rey.
The queen is the king's wife.

reír(se)   *to laugh*
La mejor medicina es reírse.
The best medicine is to laugh.

relación f.   *relationship*
No es fácil mantener una relación de larga distancia.
Maintaining a long-distance relationship isn't easy.

religión f.   *religion*
La religión ha jugado un papel importante en la historia
latinoamericana.
Religion has played an important role in Latin American history.

reloj (de pulsera) m.   *clock, wrist watch*
Llegué tarde porque mi reloj está descompuesto.
I arrived late because my watch is broken.

remedio m.   *remedy, cure*
El amor es el mejor remedio.
Love is the best cure.

remplazar   *to replace*
Necesito remplazar las baterías de mi cámara.
I need to replace my camera's batteries.

rentar   *to rent, to lease*
¿Vas a rentar un departamento?
Are you going to rent an apartment?

reparar   *to repair*
Necesitamos repararlo para seguir el viaje.
We need to repair it in order to go on with the trip.

repetir   *to repeat*
¿Puedes repetir lo que acabas de decir?
Can you repeat what you just said?

reproductor (de CD, MP3) m.   *(CD, MP3) player*
Los reproductores de MP3 se han vuelto muy populares.
MP3 players have become very popular.

reservación f.   *reservation*
La reservación está a nombre de la compañía.
The reservation is under the company's name.

reservar   *to reserve*
Hablé para reservar una mesa para cuatro ayer.
I called to reserve a table for four yesterday.

resistir   *to resist*
A veces es imposible resistir la tentación.
Sometimes temptation is impossible to resist.

respetar   *to respect*
Podríamos empezar por respetar más a la naturaleza.
We could begin by respecting nature more.

respiración f.   *breathing*
¿Sabes cómo dar respiración de boca a boca?
Do you know how to give mouth-to-mouth respiration?

respirar   *to breathe*
Es saludable respirar aire puro.
It is healthy to breathe fresh air.

responder   *to reply, to respond*
Trato de responder a los mensajes de texto tan pronto como los
recibo.
I try to reply to text messages as soon as I receive them.

respuesta f.   *answer*
No tengo una buena respuesta a tu pregunta.
I don't have a good answer for your question.

restaurante m.   *restaurant*
Queremos ir a un restaurante de comida típica.
We want to go to a traditional-food restaurant.

retraso m.   *delay*
No puedo justificar mi retraso.
I can't justify my delay.

reunir(se)   *to meet, to assemble*
Debemos reunirnos para discutir nuestro itinerario.
We must meet to discuss our itinerary.

revisar   *to review, to check*
Primero, tengo que revisar el mapa.
First, I have to check the map.

rey m.   *king*
Carlos I era rey de España y de Alemania.
Carlos I was king of Spain and Germany.

riesgo m.   *risk*
A algunas personas les encanta tomar riesgos innecesarios.
Some people really like taking unnecessary risks.

río m.   *river*
¿Podemos bañarnos en el río?
Can we bathe in the river?

risa f.   *laughter*
La risa es sana para el alma.
Laughter is healthy for the soul.

romántico/-a   *romantic*
El tango es un baile más sensual que romántico.
The tango is more a sensual than a romantic dance.

romper(se)   *to break*
Se cayó y se rompió la pierna.
She fell and broke her leg.

ropa (interior, de cama) f.   *clothes, underwear, bed linen*
No olvides empacar suficiente ropa interior.
Don't forget to pack enough underwear.

roto/-a   *broken*
Su pierna está rota.
Her leg is broken.

rubio/-a   *blond/e*
Juana tiene el pelo rubio.
Juana has blond hair.

ruido m.   *noise*
¿Qué es ese ruido espantoso?
What's that frightful noise?

ruta f.   *route*
Las rutas poco conocidas son muchas veces las más interesantes.
Little-known routes are often the most interesting.

S

sábana f.   *sheet*
¿Quiere que cambie las sábanas?
Do you want me to change the sheets?

saber (a)   *to know, to taste like*
Este café sabe a chocolate.
This coffee tastes like chocolate.

sabroso/-a   *tasty, delicious*
A todo el mundo le gusta la comida sabrosa.
Everybody likes tasty food.

sacar   *to take out, to extract*
Necesito sacar el corcho de esta botella.
I need to take out this bottle's cork.

sala (de espera) f.   *living room, (waiting room)*
Por favor espere en la sala de espera.
Please wait in the waiting room.

salario m.   *salary, wage*
Muchas veces el salario mínimo es insuficiente para cubrir nece-
sidades básicas.
Minimum wage is often insufficient to cover basic needs.

saldo (bancario) m.   *(bank) account balance*
Comprar demasiadas cosas no sería bueno para mi saldo
   bancario.
Buying too many things wouldn't be good for my account balance.

salida (del sol) f.   *exit, departure, sunrise*
Las salidas de emergencia están claramente señaladas.
The emergency exits are clearly marked.

salir   *to exit, to go out*
¿Quieres salir conmigo?
Do you want to go out with me?

saludar   *to greet*
En muchos países la gente se saluda con un beso.
In many countries people greet each other with a kiss.

secar(se)   *to dry (up)*
Necesito secar mi ropa.
I need to dry my clothes.

sección (de [no] fumar) f.   *([non]-smoking) section*
¿Prefiere la sección de fumar o de no fumar?
Do you prefer the smoking or the non-smoking section?

seco/-a   *dry*
Ya está seca tu ropa.
Your clothes are dry now.

secreto m.   *secret*
El secreto de la salsa está en la mezcla de los condimentos.
The secret of the sauce is in the condiment blend.

sed f.   *thirst*
Tengo sed.
I am thirsty.

seguir   *to follow, to continue*
Sígueme.
Follow me.

según   *according to*
Según este mapa, estamos por llegar.
According to this map, we are about to get there.

seguridad f.   *security*
Llamaré a seguridad.
I will call security.

seguro (médico, de vida, social) m.	*(medical, life) insurance,*
   medi-cal insurance, social security
¿Tienes un seguro médico?
Do you have medical insurance?

seguro/-a	*safe*
Me siento más seguro en grupo.
I feel safer in a group.

seleccionar	*to select, to pick*
Hay que seleccionar los ingredientes más frescos.
We have to select the freshest ingredients.

sembrar	*to plant*
Mi tío siembra vegetales en su huerta cada año.
My uncle plants vegetables in his vegetable garden every year.

semejante	*similar*
Este modelo es semejante pero más barato.
This model is similar but cheaper.

señal f.	*signal, sign*
Obedece todas las señales de tránsito.
Obey all the traffic signals.

sencillo/-a	*simple, easy*
Es más sencillo llegar al museo en metro.
It's easier to get to the museum on the subway.

señor(a)	*Mr., sir/Mrs., madam, lady*
Esa señora es la esposa del señor López.
That lady is Mr. López's wife.

señorita f.	*young woman, Miss*
Su hija es una señorita muy talentosa.
Their daughter is a very talented young lady.

sensual	*sensual, sensuous*
Los ritmos latinos en general son muy sensuales.
Latin rhythms in general are very sensual.

sentar(se)	*to sit down*
Siéntense, por favor.
Please, sit down.

sentido m.	*sense, meaning, direction*
Esta comedia no tiene sentido.
The comedy (play) doesn't make sense.

sentir(se) *to feel*
Me siento culpable por lo que hice.
I feel guilty for what I did.

separar(se) *to separate*
No se separen del grupo para no perderse.
Don't separate yourselves from the group so you don't get lost.

ser *to be* (as masculine noun), *being*
¿Ser o no ser? Esa es la pregunta.
To be or not to be? That is the question.

serio/-a *serious*
El SIDA es otra amenaza global muy seria.
AIDS is another very serious global threat.

seropositivo/-a *HIV positive*
En la actualidad hay más opciones médicas para las personas
  seropositivas.
Today there are more medical options for people who are HIV positive.

servicio (de mesa) m. *(table) service*
El servicio en ese hotel no es muy bueno.
The service at that hotel isn't very good.

servicios m. pl. *restrooms*
¿Puede decirme dónde están los servicios?
Can you tell me where the restrooms are?

servir(se) *to serve*
El mesero nos sirvió la comida rápidamente.
The waiter served us the food quickly.

si *if*
Si llueve no podremos ir de excursión.
If it rains we can't go on the excursion.

sí *yes*
Sí, tienes razón.
Yes, you're right.

SIDA m. *AIDS*
Encontrar una vacuna contra el SIDA es sólo una cuestión de
  tiempo.
Finding an AIDS vaccine is only a matter of time.

siempre   *always*
Siempre como pan tostado en el desayuno.
I always eat toast for breakfast.

significado m.   *meaning*
Este lugar tiene mucho significado para mí.
This place has a lot of meaning for me.

siguiente   *next, following*
Necesitamos bajar en la siguiente estación.
We need to get off at the next station.

silla f.   *chair*
La mesa del comedor tiene doce sillas.
The dining-room table has twelve chairs.

similar   *similar*
Estos modelos son similares pero éste es mucho más barato.
These models are similar but this one is a lot cheaper.

simpático/-a   *nice, friendly*
Ignacio es muy simpático.
Ignacio is very nice.

sin (embargo)   *without (nevertheless)*
No quiero ir sin ti.
I don't want to go without you.

sitio m.   *place, site*
Conozco un sitio agradable para comer.
I know a nice place to eat.

sobre   *on (top of)/(as masculine noun), envelope*
El sobre está sobre la mesa.
The envelope is on the table.

sol m.   *sun*
Los incas adoraban al sol.
The Incas worshipped the sun.

solamente   *only*
Solamente tomo café en las mañanas.
I only drink coffee in the mornings.

solicitar   *to request*
Solicitaré una visa para viajar a Cuba.
I will request a visa to travel to Cuba.

solo   *alone*
Viajar solo no es tan divertido.
Traveling alone is not as much fun.

sólo   *only*
Sólo he estado fuera del país una vez.
I've only been out of the country once.

soñar   *to dream*
¿Qué soñaste anoche?
What did you dream last night?

sonreír   *to smile*
¡Sonrían para la foto!
Smile for the picture!

sonrisa f.   *smile*
Las sonrisas son mejores que las lágrimas.
Smiles are better than tears.

sorpresa f.   *surprise*
Este viaje ha estado lleno de sorpresas.
This trip has been full of surprises.

suave   *soft, smooth*
¡Qué sábanas tan suaves!
What soft sheets!

subir(se)   *to go up, to climb*
¿Quieres subirte a la montaña rusa?
Do you want to ride the roller coaster?

sucio/-a   *dirty*
El piso de la cocina está muy sucio.
The kitchen floor is very dirty.

sudar   *to perspire, to sweat*
Cuando hago ejercicio sudo.
When I exercise I sweat.

suelo m.   *ground, floor*
La taza cayó al suelo y se rompió en mil pedazos.
The cup fell to the floor and broke into a thousand pieces.

sueño m.   *dream, sleep*
Los sueños se pueden hacer realidad.
Dreams can come true.

suerte f.   *luck*
Te deseo buena suerte.
I wish you good luck.

suficiente   *enough, sufficient*
No olvides traer suficiente agua.
Don't forget to bring enough water.

sur m.   *south*
Argentina está en el extremo sur del continente.
Argentina is in the southern-most extreme of the continent.

T

tabaco m.   *tobacco*
El mejor tabaco viene del Caribe.
The best tobacco comes from the Caribbean.

tal vez   *maybe, perhaps*
Tal vez no te guste lo que compré para ti.
Perhaps you won't like what I bought for you.

talla f.   *size (clothing)*
¿Tiene este vestido en una talla más grande?
Do you have this dress in a larger size?

taller m.   *repair shop, garage*
¿Hay un taller mecánico cerca de aquí?
Is there a garage near here?

también   *also, as well*
Agustín trabaja y estudia también.
Agustín works and studies as well.

tampoco   *neither*
La visita no fue interesante, ni divertida tampoco.
The visit was neither interesting nor fun.

taquilla f.   *box office, ticket counter*
¿Dónde está la taquilla del teatro?
Where is the theater box office?

tarifa f.   *rate, fare*
¿Cuál es la tarifa por hora?
What's the hourly rate?

tarjeta (de crédito, postal) f.   *(credit, post) card*
Mándame una tarjeta postal.
Send me a postcard.

teatro m.   *theater*
¿Quieres ir al cine o al teatro esta noche?
Do you want to go to the movies or to the theater tonight?

teclado m.   *keyboard*
Los pianos y las computadoras tienen un teclado.
Pianos and computers have a keyboard.

tela f.   *cloth*
La tela de este vestido es de muy alta calidad.
This dress's cloth is very high quality.

teléfono (celular, móvil) m.   *telephone, (cell phone)*
No olvides tu teléfono celular.
Do not forget your cell phone.

televisión f.   *television*
A pesar de tantos canales casi nunca hay nada que ver en la
    televisión.
*In spite of so many channels, there is almost never anything to watch
    on TV.*

temer   *to fear*
No le temo a nada.
I fear nothing.

templado/-a   *warm, mild*
Un día templado es ideal para una excursión larga.
A warm day is ideal for a long excursion.

temprano   *early*
Mañana saldremos muy temprano por la mañana.
Tomorrow we will leave very early in the morning.

tener (que, calor, ganas)   *to have, (to have to, to feel hot, to feel like)*
No tengo ganas de ir pero tengo que hacerlo de todos modos.
I don't feel like going but I have to anyway.

terminal (de autobuses) f.   *(bus) terminal*
¿Me puede decir dónde está la terminal de autobuses?
Can you tell me where the bus terminal is?

terminar   *to finish, to end*
Tengo que terminar mi tarea antes de salir.
I need to finish my homework before going out.

testarudo/-a   *stubborn*
A veces las personas testarudas consiguen lo que quieren.
Sometimes stubborn people get what they want.

tienda (de abarrotes) f.   *(grocery) store*
¿Dónde está la tienda de abarrotes más cercana?
Where is the nearest grocery store?

tierno/-a   *tender, young, affectionate*
Rocío tiene un corazón muy tierno.
Rocío has a tender heart.

tierra f.   *earth, soil, ground*
Los tomates necesitan buena tierra y mucho sol para crecer.
Tomatoes need good soil and a lot of sun to grow.

típico/-a   *typical*
Estas artesanías son típicas de Oaxaca.
These handcrafts are typical of Oaxaca.

tipo (de cambio) m.   *type, (exchange rate)*
¿Cuál es el tipo de cambio hoy?
What is the exchange rate today?

tocar   *to touch, to play (music)*
¿Sabes tocar un instrumento musical?
Do you know how to play a musical instrument?

todavía   *still, yet*
No estoy listo todavía.
I'm not ready yet.

todo(s)   *all, everyone, everything*
Todos quieren probar todos los platillos.
Everyone wants to try all the dishes.

tomar   *to take/to have something to eat or drink*
Toma tu sombrero y vamos a tomar una bebida cerca de la
piscina.
Take your hat and let's go have a drink by the pool.

trabajar   *to work*
¿Dónde trabajas?
Where do you work?

trabajo m.   *work, job*
Mi trabajo es peligroso.
My work is dangerous.

tradicional   *traditional*
Ese es el desayuno tradicional en España.
That's the typical breakfast in Spain.

traducir   *to translate*
Por favor tradúceme aquel anuncio.
Please translate that sign over there for me.

traer   *to bring*
No olvides traer un suéter por si hace frío.
Don't forget to bring a sweater in case it gets cold.

tráfico m.   *traffic*
El problema principal es que el tráfico de drogas es muy buen
    negocio.
The main problem is that drug trafficking is a very good business.

tranquilo/-a   *calm, peaceful*
El mar está tranquilo; podemos nadar.
The sea is calm; we can swim.

tratar (de)   *to try (to)*
Vale la pena intentarlo una vez por lo menos.
It's worth trying at least once.

tren m.   *train*
Prefiero viajar en tren que en avión.
I would rather travel by train than by plane.

trepar   *to climb, to scale*
Tendremos que trepar un poco para llegar a las ruinas.
We will have to climb a little bit to get to the ruins.

tropezar(se)   *to trip, to stumble*
Me tropecé con una piedra en el camino.
I tripped on a stone in the road.

túnel m. *tunnel*
Me asustan los túneles muy largos.
Long tunnels scare me.

turista m. & f. *tourist*
No es lo mismo ser un turista que ser un viajero.
Being a tourist is not the same as being a traveler.

U

último/-a *last*
Mi último viaje a Guatemala fue fantástico.
My last trip to Guatemala was fantastic.

una vez f. *once*
He estado en Costa Rica solamente una vez.
I have been in Costa Rica only once.

único/-a *only, unique*
Es el único país que he visitado en Centroamérica.
It's the only country I have visited in Central America.

unidad (de disco) f. *unit/(disk drive)*
¿Puede reparar la unidad de disco de mi computadora portátil?
Can you fix my laptop's disk drive?

usado/-a *worn, used*
Estos zapatos son muy cómodos porque están muy usados.
These shoes are very comfortable because they're very worn.

usar *to use*
¿Puedo usar su baño?
May I use your bathroom?

útil *useful*
Saber hablar español es muy útil.
Knowing Spanish is very useful.

V

vacaciones f. pl. *vacation, holiday*
¿A dónde van a ir de vacaciones?
Where are you going on your vacation?

vacío/-a   *empty*
El avión estaba casi vacío.
The plane was almost empty.

valioso/-a   *valuable*
No traigas nada valioso.
Don't bring anything valuable.

valor m.   *value/courage, bravery*
A veces hay que mostrar valor.
Sometimes you have to show courage.

varios   *several, various*
Vamos a visitar varios museos en Madrid.
We are going to visit several museums in Madrid.

vaso m.   *(drinking) glass*
¿Quieres un vaso de agua?
Do you want a glass of water?

vecindario m.   *neighborhood*
El hotel está en un vecindario agradable.
The hotel is in a nice neighborhood.

vegetariano/-a   *vegetarian*
Soy vegetariano.
I am a vegetarian.

vehículo m.   *vehicle*
Necesitamos un vehículo rápido para llegar pronto.
We need a fast vehicle to get there quickly.

velocidad f.   *speed*
Respeta el límite de velocidad.
Respect the speed limit.

vender   *to sell*
¿Dónde venden artesanías?
Where do they sell handcrafts?

venir   *to come*
Ven a almorzar con nosotros.
Come have lunch with us.

venta f.   *sale*
Esta casa está a la venta.
This house is for sale.

ventana f. *window*
Cierra la ventana por favor
Close the window please.

ventilador m. *fan*
Tengo calor, ¿puedes encender el ventilador?
I'm hot; can you turn on the fan?

ver *to see, to watch*
No me gusta ver la televisión.
I don't like to watch television.

verdad f. *truth*
Dime la verdad.
Tell me the truth.

verificar *to verify*
Los agentes de inmigración están ahí para verificar la identidad
de los viajeros.
Immigration agents are there to verify travelers' identities.

vestir(se) *to dress, to get dressed*
Luis siempre se viste muy bien.
Luis always dresses very well.

veraz *truthful*
En los negocios, como en el amor, es mejor ser veraz.
In business, as in love, it's better to be truthful.

vez f. *time (instance)*
Generalmente, se come tres veces al día.
In general, people eat three times a day.

viajar *to travel*
Me encanta viajar en tren.
I love to travel by train.

vida f. *life*
Todo el mundo quiere una buena vida.
Everybody wants a good life.

videograbadora f. *video recorder*
Olvidé mi videograbadora en casa.
I forgot my video recorder at home.

videojuego m.   *video/computer game*
Los videojuegos son muy populares hoy en día.
Video games are very popular these days.

virus m.   *virus*
No hay una cura efectiva contra los virus.
There isn't an effective cure against viruses.

visa (de negocios) f.   *(business) visa*
No se necesita una visa para viajar a España o a México.
You don't need a visa to travel to Spain or Mexico.

visitar   *to visit*
Vale la pena visitar las ruinas de Palenque.
The Palenque ruins are worth visiting.

vivir   *to live*
¿Alguien vive aquí?
Does anybody live here?

volar   *to fly*
Vuelo seguido a Monterrey por negocios.
I fly to Monterrey often for business.

volver(se)   *to return, to become*
Quiero volver a Ecuador pronto.
I want to return to Ecuador soon.

vuelta f.   *turn/tour/return*
Da vuelta a la derecha en la próxima esquina.
Turn right at the next corner.

Y

y   *and*
Compré un vestido y un par de zapatos
I bought a dress and a pair of shoes.

ya   *already*
¿Ya has visto la exposición de Picasso?
Have you already seen the Picasso exhibition?

Z

zócalo m.   *central/main square*
En el zócalo hay una estatua del héroe nacional.
On the main square there is a statue of the national hero.

zoológico m.   *zoo*
¿Quieres visitar el zoológico?
Do you want to visit the zoo?

zurdo/-a   *left-handed*
Tristán es zurdo.
Tristan is left-handed.

Category Section

LA FAMILIA	f.	THE FAMILY
abuelo/-a	m./f.	*grandfather/mother*
cuñado/-a	m./f.	*brother/sister-in-law*
esposo/-a	m./f.	*husband/wife, spouse*
hermano/-a	m./f.	*brother/sister*
hijo/-a	m./f.	*son/daughter*
madre	f.	*mother*
madrina	f.	*godmother*
nieto/-a	m./f.	*grandson/daughter*
nuera	f.	*daughter-in-law*
padre	m.	*father*
padrino	m.	*godfather*
primo/-a	m./f.	*cousin*
sobrino/-a	m./f.	*nephew/niece*
suegro/-a	m./f.	*father/mother-in-law*
tío/-a	m./f.	*uncle/aunt*
yerno	m.	*son-in-law*

TIEMPO	m.	TIME
año	m.	*year*
anoche		*last night*
ayer		*yesterday*

hora	f.	*hour*
hoy		*today*
mañana	f.	*morning/tomorrow*
medianoche	f.	*midnight*
mediodía	m.	*noon*
noche	f.	*evening*
tarde	f.	*afternoon/late*

DÍAS DE LA SEMANA	f. pl.	***DAYS OF THE WEEK***
lunes		*Monday*
martes		*Tuesday*
miércoles		*Wednesday*
jueves		*Thursday*
viernes		*Friday*
sábado		*Saturday*
domingo		*Sunday*
semana (próxima)	f.	*(next) week*

MESES	m. pl.	***MONTHS***
enero		*January*
febrero		*February*
marzo		*March*
abril		*April*
mayo		*May*
junio		*June*
julio		*July*
agosto		*August*
septiembre		*September*
octubre		*October*

noviembre		*November*
diciembre		*December*

LAS ESTACIONES	m. pl.	***THE SEASONS***
primavera	f.	*spring*
verano	m.	*summer*
otoño	m.	*autumn*
invierno	m.	*winter*

EL CUERPO	m.	***THE BODY***
barbilla	f.	*chin*
boca	f.	*mouth*
brazo	m.	*arm*
cabeza	f.	*head*
cadera	f.	*hip*
cara	f.	*face*
ceja	f.	*eyebrow*
cerebro	m.	*brain*
cintura	f.	*waist*
codo	m.	*elbow*
corazón	m.	*heart*
costilla	f.	*rib*
cuello	m.	*neck*
dedo (del pie)	m.	*finger, toe*
diente	m.	*tooth*
espalda	f.	*back*
estómago	m.	*stomach*
garganta	f.	*throat*
hombro	m.	*shoulder*

hueso	m.	*bone*
labio	m.	*lip*
lengua	f.	*tongue*
mandíbula	f.	*jaw*
mano	f.	*hand*
nalgas	f. pl.	*buttocks*
nariz	f.	*nose*
ojo	m.	*eye*
oreja	f.	*ear*
panza	f.	*belly, stomach*
pecho	m.	*chest, breast*
pelo	m.	*hair*
pene	m.	*penis*
pie	m.	*foot*
pierna	f.	*leg*
pulmón	m.	*lung*
rodilla	f.	*knee*
sangre	f.	*blood*
tobillo	m.	*ankle*
vagina	f.	*vagina*
SALUD	f.	***HEALTH***
alergia	f.	*allergy*
ampolla	f.	*blister*
analgésico	m.	*painkiller*
ardor	m.	*burning pain*
calmante	f.	*painkiller*
catarro	m.	*cold (illness)*
cirugía	f.	*surgery*

cirujano	m. & f.	*surgeon*
comezón	f.	*itch*
consulta (externa)	f.	*medical examination/ out-patient clinic*
consultorio médico	m.	*doctor's office*
convalecer		*to recover*
curación	f.	*treatment, cure*
curar		*to cure, to heal, to treat*
curita	f.	*Band-Aid*
desmayarse		*to faint*
diagnóstico	m.	*diagnosis*
diarrea	f.	*diarrhea*
dislocar		*to dislocate*
doler		*to hurt, to ache*
dolor (de cabeza)	m.	*pain, headache*
dosis	f.	*dose*
enfermarse		*to get sick*
enfermedad	f.	*disease, illness*
enfermero/-a	m./f.	*nurse*
enfermo/-a		*sick*
estreñimiento	m.	*constipation*
fiebre	f.	*fever*
gripe	f.	*flu*
hemorragia	f.	*hemorrhage*
herida	f.	*wound, injury*
hinchado/-a		*swollen*
indigestión	f.	*indigestion*
infarto	m.	*heart attack*
inflamación	f.	*swelling*

inhalador	m.	*inhaler*
intoxicación (alimenticia)	f.	*(food) poisoning*
jaqueca	f.	*migraine*
jarabe (para la tos)	m.	*(cough) syrup*
jeringa	f.	*syringe*
lastimado/-a		*hurt, injured*
lastimar(se)		*to hurt (oneself)*
lesionado/-a		*hurt, injured*
lesionar(se)		*to injure (oneself)*
malestar	m.	*discomfort*
medicina (general)	f.	*medicine, general practice*
médico	m. & f.	*doctor*
moretón	m.	*bruise*
picadura (de dientes, de insecto)	f.	*sting (cavity, insect bite)*
picazón	f.	*itch*
primeros auxilios	m. pl.	*first aid*
quemadura (de sol)	f.	*(sun) burn*
receta (médica)	f.	*prescription*
resfriado	m.	*cold (illness)*
retortijón	m.	*(stomach) cramp*
saludable		*healthy*
sangrar		*to bleed*
sano/-a		*healthy*
torcedura	f.	*sprain*
tos	f.	*cough*
toser		*to cough*
urticaria	f.	*rash, hives*
venda	f.	*bandage*

NÚMEROS	m. pl.	NUMBERS
cero		*zero*
uno		*one*
dos		*two*
tres		*three*
cuatro		*four*
cinco		*five*
seis		*six*
siete		*seven*
ocho		*eight*
nueve		*nine*
diez		*ten*
once		*eleven*
doce		*twelve*
trece		*thirteen*
catorce		*fourteen*
quince		*fifteen*
dieciséis		*sixteen*
diecisiete		*seventeen*
dieciocho		*eighteen*
diecinueve		*nineteen*
veinte		*twenty*
veintiuno		*twenty-one*
veintidós		*twenty-two*
treinta		*thirty*
treinta y uno		*thirty-one*
treinta y dos		*thirty-two*
cuarenta		*forty*
cincuenta		*fifty*

sesenta		*sixty*
setenta		*seventy*
ochenta		*eighty*
noventa		*ninety*
cien		*one hundred*
ciento uno		*one hundred one*
ciento dos		*one hundred two*
doscientos		*two hundred*
trescientos		*three hundred*
cuatrocientos		*four hundred*
quinientos		*five hundred*
seiscientos		*six hundred*
setecientos		*seven hundred*
ochocientos		*eight hundred*
novecientos		*nine hundred*
mil		*one thousand*
dos mil		*two thousand*
cien mil		*one hundred thousand*
millón	m.	*million*
dos millones		*two million*

PALABRAS INTERROGATIVAS	f. pl.	**QUESTION WORDS**
¿cómo?		*how?*
¿cuál(es)?		*which?*
¿cuándo?		*when?*
¿cuánto?		*how much?*
¿cuántos/-as?		*how many?*
¿dónde?		*where?*
¿por qué?		*why?*

DEPORTES	m. pl.	*SPORTS*
baloncesto	m.	*basketball*
béisbol	m.	*baseball*
boliche/bolos	m./m. pl.	*bowling*
caña (de pescar)	f.	*(fishing) rod*
cancha (de tenis)	f.	*(tennis) court*
ciclismo	m.	*cycling*
corrida (de toros)	f.	*bullfight*
equitación	f.	*horse riding*
esquí acuático	m.	*waterskiing*
esquiar		*to ski*
fútbol (americano)	m.	*soccer, football*
lucha libre	f.	*wrestling*
natación	f.	*swimming*
tenis	m.	*tennis*

TIENDAS	f. pl.	*STORES*
barbería	f.	*barber shop*
cafetería	f.	*cafeteria*
carnicería	f.	*butcher shop*
farmacia	f.	*pharmacy, drugstore*
ferretería	f.	*hardware store*
florería	f.	*flower shop*
joyería	f.	*jewelry store*
lavandería	f.	*laundromat*
librería	f.	*bookstore*
panadería	f.	*bakery*
papelería	f.	*stationers, office supply store*

peluquería	f.	*hairdresser*
sastrería	f.	*tailor shop*
supermercado	m.	*supermarket*
tintorería	f.	*dry cleaner's*
zapatería	f.	*shoe store*

COLORES	m. pl.	***COLORS***
amarillo		*yellow*
anaranjado		*orange*
azul (claro, oscuro)		*(light, dark) blue*
blanco		*white*
café		*brown*
gris		*grey*
marrón		*brown*
morado		*purple*
negro		*black*
rojo		*red*
rosa		*pink*
verde		*green*

ANIMALES	m. pl.	***ANIMALS***
abeja	f.	*bee*
araña	f.	*spider*
burro/-a	m./f.	*donkey*
caballo/yegua	m./f.	*horse/mare*
cabra	f.	*goat*
cerdo/-a	m./f.	*pig, pork*
conejo/-a	m./f.	*rabbit*
cucaracha	f.	*cockroach*

cuervo	m.	*crow*
culebra	f.	*water snake*
gallo/gallina	m./f.	*hen/rooster*
gato/-a	m./f.	*cat*
hormiga	f.	*ant*
lagarto	m.	*lizard*
lobo/-a	m./f.	*wolf*
mono/-a	m./f.	*monkey*
mosca	f.	*fly*
mosquito	m.	*mosquito*
oso/-a	m./f.	*bear*
oveja	f.	*sheep*
pájaro	m.	*bird*
palomo/-a	m./f.	*pigeon/dove*
pato/-a	m./f.	*duck*
pavo/-a	m./f.	*turkey*
perro/-a	m./f.	*dog*
puerco/-a	m./f.	*pig, pork*
rana	f.	*frog*
ratón	m.	*mouse*
tiburón	m.	*shark*
toro/vaca	m./f.	*bull/cow*
víbora	f.	*snake*

Vocabulary Tips and Cognates

Cognates are words that derive from a common ancestor language. Most words in Spanish and many words in English come from Latin or Greek. As a result, there are a lot of words in English that are cognates of words in Spanish; most are easily recognizable. Since changes are slight and predictable, you can quickly expand your vocabulary in Spanish by taking note of the following:

1. Some words are the same in both languages (except that their pronunciation may vary): color, crisis, drama, error, general, horror, probable, tropical, . . .
2. Some words add an extra vowel to the English word: cli-ente, evidente, ignorante, importante, parte, artista, pianista, problema, programa, contacto, perfecto, líquido, . . .[1]
3. Many words ending in -ty in English end in -tad or -dad in Spanish: facultad, libertad, curiosidad, sociedad, eternidad, capacidad, realidad, claridad, . . .
4. Many words ending in -y in English end in -ía, -ia, or -io (depending on gender, see below): compañía, geografía, historia, farmacia, diccionario, ordinario, . . .[2]
5. Words that end in -tion in English generally end in -ción in Spanish: nación, administración, acción, fricción, sección, emoción, combinación, contribución, . . .
6. Words that end in -ous in English often end in -oso in Spanish: generoso, famoso, precioso, delicioso, tedioso, contagioso, curioso, escandaloso, religioso, . . .

---

[1] Please don't make the error, often parodied in movies, of thinking that adding an "o" at the end of every word in a sentence makes it sound like Spanish. In fact, native Spanish speakers will likely consider this rude.

[2] In a few cases, cognates don't have exactly the same meaning in Spanish as they do in English: *policía* means "police" in Spanish; policy should be translated as *política*.